I HATED SCHOOL UNTIL I FIGURED IT OUT

By

Dr. Ralph F. Murphy II

Maven Scholars Consulting LLC

www.mavenscholar.com

mavenscholar@outlook.com

Edited by Madison D., Write My Wrongs LLC

Book Cover by Edward Burgess, Muse Digital Media

Printed in the United States of America

Distributed by CreateSpace

First printing 2018

ISBN 978-0-692-08671-1

MAVEN

SCHOLAR CONSULTING

Thank you to family and friends for the support along the way to complete this book. Also, special thanks to Edward Burgess (Muse Digital Media), Marquis Maines (Marquis Maines Designs), Nathaniel Austin for the logo design, Kenneth "Shujaa" Rice, and Kevin Coburn. Above all, special thanks to my wife.

"The more that you read, the more things you will know…"

- Dr. Seuss

TABLE OF CONTENTS

INTRODUCTION

Without a doubt, the education system equips people with the knowledge to become adults capable of sustaining a quality life. Although global ratings reveal some educational systems are better than others, they—K-12 and higher education—all serve as vital resources to enhance economic growth and stability worldwide. Education is needed to obtain job advancement or the career goals one aspires to obtain. For these reasons, it's important to note few people comfortably survive without some sort of diploma, college degree, or professional certificate. Yet, navigating through these systems to obtain success is not easy, and often, education systems are feared and viewed as a barrier to success which causes many people to hate school.

To publicly announce hating school is taboo, awkward, politically incorrect, or however you want to describe it; but in many instances, school is considered a waste of time and money. In fact, the obstacles impeding student success can be psychologically damaging.

There are many variables that affect learning in and out of the classroom, no matter the education system that must be accounted for.

For starters, just like many students today, I hated waking up early in the morning. The school lunch was terrible. I always felt like nobody understood me. I hated the dress code. And just like others, I resented many of my teachers and administrators. Yes, I had dreams of being a star athlete at a major university, playing basketball, football, or running track. No, it didn't happen.

Next, I hated the fear of the unknown as an under-educated, first-generation, poor college student trying to adapt to college life alone. I hated the feelings of anxiety, depression, and psychological tension of the war within myself to be successful. At times, by being under-educated, I didn't understand college lectures, couldn't afford to buy books for class, and lacked the ability to avoid distractions negatively affecting my college success. But that's of course, until I figured it out!

If you've picked this narrative up, it's more than likely you either hated or currently hate school, too! Although my resentment for school was monumental, my affinity for knowledge and growth as a life-long learner is greater. Therefore, this is not propaganda to destroy, dismantle, or instigate any political action toward the education system; however, this is an impactful narrative to guide learners navigating through education and life simultaneously. Through the worst of times and the best of times—experiencing teacher strikes or party celebrations for graduating—I hated school. I can't say it enough. This passion of resentment ignited my cognitive ability to orchestrate strategies at every education level. I saw education through a lens that could've made me more competitive than Michael Jordan or Kobe Bryant, National Basketball Association players and world champions.

Knowing that, this book is written through a strategist lens comparable to John Wooden, Phil Jackson, John Madden, or Bill Belichick, championship professional basketball and football coaches. Looking back on the experiences met while transitioning through the education systems, I called more audibles—Omaha—than Peyton Manning, famous National Football League quarterback. Through trial and error, I learned that back-up plans to back-up plans became a requisite for life, and this was my foundation for figuring out how to be successful in school.

The experiences within this text reveal the undiscussables impeding high school and college graduation. Stories include struggling to be socially accepted, failing courses, and making bad decisions in and out of the classroom. While these moments can be dreadful they increased my mental ability and strengthened shortcomings to becoming a better person every day. Even more, these moments helped me figure out how to hone my skills and learn how to learn.

As time progressed, I figured out how to strategically maneuver past diversions and make decisions circumventing situations that would've altered the trajectory of my life at every level of education. Therefore, my shared personal learning experiences should be analyzed from the perspective of the reader for critical evaluation and assessment. Most importantly, these experiences do not assert there is one way to navigate through the education system, but rather a combination of strategies utilized in tandem at the discretion of students seeking to graduate and enter the workforce.

By the time you finish this book, you will figure it out too! You will know how to hone your skills and learn how to learn, as well. Also, by doing these things, I hope you figure out school from your vantage point. It all begins with self-assessment.

Take a moment and meditate on this question: how many things can you think of to occupy your time and mind beyond the classroom? Consequently, whenever school is compared to video game systems, posting on social media, browsing the internet, shopping, playing sports, listening to music, visiting friends, sleeping, or just doing absolutely nothing, learning inside a classroom is considered an inconvenience.

Given the infinite distractions, it's clear some students are simply uninterested in learning. Assuming students today understood the impact of delayed gratification— the time it takes to graduate from high school and college— and valued learning a disconnect between students and learning would not exist.

Subsequently, if a disconnect did not exist, students today would appreciate learning opportunities and show the scholastic achievement early ancestors of all ethnicities dreamed of. In contrast, the disconnect is shown through high numbers of poor K-12 school systems overwhelmed with low test scores, low attendance, and low graduation reports, in addition to high suspension rates. At the same time, national research summaries show low rates of high school to college transitions. Even worse, retention and degree completion rates within higher education are abysmal, and applicant pools for qualified employees to fill workforce vacancies are lowering.

The text above led my thoughts as I developed the concept for this book. I shared my ideas with high school students, college students, teachers, college professors, college presidents, community organizers, friends, and family members. They all contributed to the focus of this narrative by repeatedly asking the following questions: First, "is it possible for someone with a doctorate degree to resent school so much?" Second, "how can you be considered a scholar in the academy and not like school?" Then they asked, "if you hated school so much, why not drop out of high school, better yet, why go to college?" And the resounding question: "what exactly did you figure out about school?"

Well, in the past decade, I figured out educators, students, and community organizers—the learning community—need a truthful illustration of how to maneuver around barriers in and out of the classroom. Due to growing challenges within the education system, it's imperative I share memories coupled with conventional strategies to be used while matriculating through high school and college. At the same time, these strategies will help learners mature as adults, serving as a guide for current and future students. Therefore, after reading this book, you too will have the information needed to figure out school too.

"Does the walker choose the path, or the path the walker?"

— Garth Nix

1

Learning Pains

A FRESH FADE: CHECK! Sideburns evenly lined up, with a double-loop part design on the left: check! Dark blue khaki pants ironed with even, crisp creases: check! New white polo shirt: check! All black sneakers that could be mistaken for dress shoes: check! Brand-new book bag filled with pens, pencils, and a five-subject notebook with folders: check!

It was another sunny day cruising to school in mom's drop-top. As they arrived, Ralph jumped out, slapping high-fives and fist-bumping friends as the cheerleaders stood at the entrance of the door, chanting his name—"Give me an 'R!'"

While walking into the school, a yardstick slapped the desk, and Mrs. Harris's voice sounded off like a bullhorn. "Ralph, wake up! And it

would behoove you to stop snoring in my class, this desk is not your bed."
Just like that, the dream was over, and Ralph crashed back to reality.

Mrs. Harris, the sixth-grade honors language arts and social studies
teacher at Superior Elementary School, was a stickler on class rules,
especially students falling asleep in her class. "Okay, I'm up, Mrs. Harris.
Since I'm finished with my work, may I go to the restroom?" asked Ralph.

She replied, "You have five minutes. Take the pass, the clock starts
now."

As he took the pass and walked out the classroom door, he muttered
under his breath, "You better not wake me up like that again, what's wrong
with you?"

The class laughed, prompting Mrs. Harris to snap, "What'd you say,
young man?"

Fearing further discipline, he quickly closed the door and skipped
down the hallway before she could get out from behind her desk and call
him back to the classroom. Hearing her heels click on the tile floor, he
quickly hid around the corner fifteen feet away, until he heard her go back
into the classroom and close the door.

He let out a quick sigh. *That was a close call*, he thought. A break to
catch some fresh air was needed. Mrs. Harris's class was always quieter

than a church mouse, so a student couldn't help but fall asleep from time to time when there was no more work to do. While it might seem as if Ralph was giving Mrs. Harris a hard time, this was actually his favorite class.

She not only taught students how to write and comprehend literature—she created a learning environment focusing on self-control and respect for peace within silence. And according to Nerburn, "silence is the sign of a perfect equilibrium; it's developing the absolute poise or balance of body, mind, and spirit." Besides, silence creates a peace for students to hear themselves think without distractions. In her class, this silence prompted thinking, which was how thoughts became fluid expressions transmitted from pen to paper.

After a few weeks in her class, Ralph became so immersed in literature that he wanted his writing to flow like the Nile River. Because of this, his attention shifted from fashion, music, and athletics to reading. It was because literature was peaceful. He could read, write, and lose himself in the concepts drawn by various authors. He started wanting everyone to see how well he could read and write. He began standing up in Sunday church services, reading verses out loud that were usually read by adults.

At the same time, he'd have conversations with friends and teachers about how his life compared to the novels and biographies being read in

11

class. In addition to the novels and biographies, he also read the lyrics to the tunes he listened to daily. Words became life as Ralph wrote poems, raps, songs, and stories both in and out of the classroom.

Later, it became clear that words were his learning symbol when he wrote and recited a speech on leadership for Martin Luther King Jr. Day at Superior Elementary School, in addition to preparing a positive rap song with classmates. The speech was for a nonviolent literacy competition between nominated sixth-grade leaders—Ralph and another student, Orane McDonald, were the finalists. There were two sessions: a.m. and p.m. programs. Ralph was up first. He approached the microphone as if he had already won the oratorical contest, calmly beginning, "As the oldest of four boys, I am a leader in school and at home…"

At the end of the speech, the crowd applauded. Ralph smiled and went to his seat, while Orane strutted with a purpose to the podium. He grabbed the microphone and thunderously said, "I am a leader!" From that moment on, it was over. It was like Dr. King had spoken through the mic himself!

Ralph looked around the room, saw the attentiveness Orane's forceful presentation garnered, and took notes for when it was time to do the speech for the second time in the afternoon program. And it didn't work. The cadence was off. A lesson in preparation was learned at this moment, for next time. It was a unanimous decision, Orane won the competition.

Nonetheless, Ralph collaborated with other classmates, DoJuan and Steve, forming a rap group and writing lyrics for peace and nonviolence. They harmonized like Bone Thugs-N-Harmony while rapping, "If we could teach the whole wide world to live in peace and harmony, if we could teach the whole wide world to be like King, like King." At the end of each performance, they received standing ovations. For Ralph, this day was monumental.

After this experience, it was undeniably clear—Ralph understood the cadence and rhythm for articulating thoughts to paper and restating them in ways other people could understand. From here, he developed a positive reputation and garnered the respect from other teachers and the principal as a leader in the school.

But while he flourished in language arts and social studies, math and science became harder and harder—more so because of the inconsistency in teachers for math and science subjects. Mrs. Harris taught every day, but because the original teacher for math and science was no longer teaching after the first few weeks of class, multiple months with various substitute teachers affected his learning in these subjects.

Sadly, this sixth-grade honors math and science class didn't receive consistent teaching. The frustration mounted as each substitute came in with a new teaching strategy every day. Instead of lashing out and doing things to get suspended, Ralph disengaged from math and science learning modules. In the end, he thought there was no point in learning something one way on Monday and another by Wednesday.

Due to the confusion among the teachers instructing math and science in sixth grade, Ralph became under-skilled per grade-level requirements in those subjects. As a result, he focused even more on language arts and social studies. Almost halfway through the year—December—a new teacher arrived full-time; however, it was too late! Even worse, due to upcoming test preparation, the information was rushed and skimmed through, plus the pace was too fast. Everything became a blur. Sadly, the gap in math and science instruction would hinder his learning ability to master foundational concepts per grade learning requirements.

Consequently, moving on to junior high school would show how much his inconsistent math and science instruction would affect his success. In fact, for the first time in school, he encountered major academic woes. Because he was in honors classes in sixth grade, Ralph was placed in honors classes in junior high. This was a major mistake! The honors classes moved at a pace that was too fast, and the cadence of the learning sequence in math and science was far too advanced. Finding the rhythm to understand the concepts for algebra and geometry equations was too hard. At the same time, the pace for learning chemistry and biology was even faster. Whether it was math or science, he was always 200 yards behind in a 100-yard dash.

Although he had As in language arts and social studies, he failed multiple math and science tests with Fs, an unacceptable grade per honor student standards. Failing grades showed his inability to reach the learning pace of other classmates, and as a result, he was removed from all honors classes in the second quarter. Rather than crying or feeling embarrassed, a sense of relief and joy overcame him instantly.

In fact, this was the best way to restore his confidence in learning: by removing the pressure of upholding a scholastic achievement standard he was incapable of at this time. Instead of being overwhelmed with thoughts of seeking 4.0 to 5.0 grade point averages, receiving 3.0s each quarter was better than good enough—it was excellent. There was no pressure to learn at a fast pace, and school had become enjoyable again.

The math problems were still challenging, but not overwhelming. Instead of taking two hours or more to understand homework outside of class, now it would only take thirty minutes to one hour; because of this, his assignment and test grades transitioned from Ds and Fs to Bs and Cs. The same thing happened with science. The same teachers taught the classes, and they slowed the cadence of learning based on the abilities of the students. Had this not occurred, Ralph would've failed seventh grade. With his confidence growing academically, he became more self-conscious socially, and more comfortable with who he was becoming as a young teenager.

By the time eighth grade came, Ralph's confidence elevated his ability to get back to his strengths: reading and writing. Although he was no longer in honors classes, he was recognized by many teachers as a stellar writer. He researched information and wrote about the O.J. Simpson trial, in addition to writing a book report on Thurgood Marshall and Jesse Owens. Those writing compositions solidified him as a young scholar, and he was routinely recommended to write in different contests. Additionally, his participation in athletic programs helped him set up a notable reputation among friends, teachers, and principals. That year, the middle school won championship trophies in football, basketball, and track and field.

To Ralph, the greatest part of winning the championships was knowing the sacrifices that needed to be made, physically and psychologically, to prepare for first place. It was building the mental ability to learn how to win and how to lose respectfully. It was the preparation for gaining strength and endurance. It was the ability to overcome adversity and hard times. It was developing an understanding of teamwork and recognizing the attributes within other winners. It was knowing that hard work and dedication builds the perseverance and character needed to overcome the obstacles standing between the person and the reward.

On the other hand, it was learning to show the teachers the same respect as the coaches. It was knowing when to talk and when to listen. It was learning how to take directions and how to avoid making the same mistakes repeatedly. Most importantly, for Ralph, it was developing a first-place mindset toward academics that compelled him to excel by using words as a learning symbol as he transitioned to high school.

"Always live your truth. That way no one can use your truth against you…People can slander you all day, but no judgement or opinion formed against you shall prosper when you Live Your Truth."

\-   Charlamagne Tha God

2

Growing Pains

OVER THE SUMMER, RALPH HEARD HORROR STORIES ABOUT HIGH SCHOOL. The bullying, social acceptance pressure, and being a part of the "in-crowd." So, before classes started, he developed a **"going against the grain"** mindset, and this would single-handedly be the most important attribute he created before school started. **"Going against the grain"** was a mental tactic he used to let others know he had a mind of his own. Furthermore, no matter what people said, did, or tried to do, it would not faze him or alter his thoughts. Ralph believed he couldn't be peer pressured to do anything if he could outsmart others tactfully. It was imperative others viewed him differently and embrace the identity he was creating. Most importantly, **"going against the grain"** was daring to be positively different!

For instance, if everybody referred to Michael Jordan as the best NBA player of all-time, Ralph would argue Bill Russell was better because he had more championship rings. If friends wore blue jeans, he'd purposely wear black jeans to stand out. If everybody was rooting for the Dallas Cowboys NFL team, he'd support the opposing team.

This mindset later transitioned to not having a baby in high school, not committing a crime resulting in jail time, not doing drugs, not picking fights, not being bullied or bullying others, and not joining a gang. This also meant not joining large crowds of people, and by doing this, he felt no pressure to be accepted by anyone. In fact, Ralph was fine with having one friend, the same friend since elementary—DoJuan.

Even more, this mindset was about embracing truths early in life. He understood his family was not wealthy and could not afford to buy expensive name-brand clothes, shoes, and video game systems. He knew he came from a family of people who worked hard to make a living and not a family involved in dangerous activities. It was because of this mindset he showed strong characteristics toward self-approval.

This mind set was just the beginning of the many remarkable things to follow. Because of the strong mindset he developed, he began with the end in mind, the next move after high school graduation. Shaw High School consisted of two years of math, science, English, and elective courses, in addition to two more years with a student-selected vocational pathway for a job readiness credential upon graduation. Pathway choices were cosmetology, autobody, fire tech, culinary, criminal justice, or computer-aided drafting. Rather than focus on pathways for jobs later in life, he was focused on how to become a professional athlete.

At this time, Shaw High School was considered an athletic powerhouse with nationally recruited Division I basketball and football players in grades ahead; knowing this, Ralph figured it would only be a matter of time before a scout saw him too, but everything must go according to the plan. First, excel in courses that have majority reading and writing assignments. Next, always remember to get nothing lower than a B in elective courses such as gym, computers, and college success courses. Most importantly, get better in math and science classes. Ask for help or clearer instruction from the teachers.

Freshman year was a breeze. Ralph was a well-liked young man who did his best academically and didn't disrespect teachers. That's the golden ticket—everybody likes a respectable student! At the same time, he was making waves and getting noticed for playing basketball. Looking ahead, a 3.0 grade point average for two consecutive years would be easier than imagined given the same teachers would be teaching the same classes two years in a row—Mrs. Crawford taught English, Mr. Harvey taught math, and Mrs. Coffey taught science.

Report Card Example. Exhibit 1

English	A
Math	C
Science	C
History	B
Computer	B
Spanish	B
Gym	A
Grade Point Average	**3.0**

This figure illustrates how students can strategically map out a 3.0 grade point average based on a seven-class schedule. Each grade has a numeric value that is calculated to figure out the grade point average; A= 4, B= 3, C=2, D=1, and F=0.

The 3.0 was achieved by adding the letter grades' numeric value to 21 points and dividing it by the number 7, the number of classes taken.

Remembering his chaotic sixth-grade experience, he welcomed having consistency in core subjects for tenth grade. Ralph knew the teachers' personalities, their cadence for teaching, teaching methods, their expectations, grading scales, and their home and class assignment workloads. All the stars were lining up—two more years to go until college.

Unfortunately, before he could get a grasp on life, uncontrollable catastrophes happened all at once. It was like a scene from a movie on the big screen—someone on the slopes of the Colorado Rockies yelled "Timberrrrrr," and the avalanche poured all over him. The housing market crashed, and massive lay-offs affected his family drastically. Financially, they were at rock bottom. At this instance, his dream of using athletic stardom to financially support the family became a fantasy.

After school, Ralph worked two-jobs, a grocery store bagger and school cleaner to help with the bills. Somedays he'd miss athletic practice, which meant less playing time in football or basketball games, which also meant fewer recruiting opportunities for colleges. On the other hand, missing work meant less money. Trying to juggle two-jobs, athletics, and school became more of a nuisance than solving the problem.

It was in this moment Ralph understood vividly that obtaining a credential for a specific skill or degree(s) from a university was the most important accomplishment beyond high school. To make matters worse, as sophomore year came to an end, the teachers went on strike, protesting changes to the union contract. Not knowing what teachers or vocational programs would be available after the teacher union strike ended put all the students in a precarious situation. It was at this time that students had to carefully evaluate trade and skill programs to strategize options that presented opportunities for a higher quality of life after graduation.

Law enforcement wasn't a big draw for Ralph, but out of all the pathways, Criminal Justice had a degree track at major universities. So, with pressure mounting from all directions, he took a leap of faith and chose Criminal Justice as the two-year pathway starting his junior year.

The teacher was Commander Copeland, a retired police officer with years of experience helping students transition from high school to college then into the workforce. Even better, his class consisted of reading, writing, and studying the concepts of law and policing. College became more of a possibility as Commander lined up college trips for the upcoming weeks to the University of Toledo and Central State University. This was his big break! Had it not been for Commander Copeland, he might have never known how to select a college. Prior to the road trip, Commander Copeland prepped the class on the importance of college trips and reasons why taking these trips are a big deal.

"For starters, not all students get a chance to step foot on a college campus, let alone get accepted and graduate from one. The staff that'll be involved on the tours and the information shared in the sessions are led by key people, so listen closely."

Then, a classmate jokingly shouted, "But Commander, what if my mom or dad can't afford to pay for me to go to college? Aren't these universities for rich people?" He replied, "Universities have scholarships and grants many of you qualify for. They'll talk about financial aid and how to complete the process, so pay attention."

This information was a major sign Ralph had made the best decision of his young life to sign up for the criminal justice pathway. Earlier in the year he shared with Commander the travesties affecting his family; therefore, it was good for him to know scholarships and federal financial aid together help economically challenged—poor—students fund their college education.

From there on, Ralph approached college trips as business trips. He paid attention to everything: campus tour information, new dorms versus old dorms, recreation centers, public transportation, city life where the college was located, and the nearest shopping malls. He also looked for restaurants, college night life, athletic programs, student organizations, scholarship opportunities available once enrolled in the college, and most importantly, the professional careers of the professors teaching in the Criminal Justice department. Their professional careers alluded to their connections and ability to help Ralph obtain his degree and a career after college.

With Commander reiterating the potential career opportunities for the future, college was surely creeping up fast; but Ralph was still in high school, and it was highly important to keep a balanced high school lifestyle. This would include close friends he and DoJuan would later call "The Squad"—a group of friends that enjoyed having fun, staying out of trouble, partying, and that placed an emphasis on graduating from high school.

Whether or not it was sitting around listening to music, going to the movies, or going out to eat, it was important to have fun and be around positive, like-minded teenagers. As junior year flew by faster than a G5 jet, there's one thing The Squad continued to talk about, imitating Ms. Beverly Bright-Lloyd's, the senior class principal's, voice, "We only have one more year of high school, and then we're off to the real world, people."

Senior year arrived, but he hadn't taken the SAT or ACT test; either one is needed for scholarships and for college course placement. In a panic, he registered for the Saturday SAT test at 8:00 a.m. in mid-October—the same Saturday morning after the Friday night homecoming football game! Rather than rescheduling the test, he believed he could play football Friday night, then wake up by 6:00 a.m. Saturday morning to be ready for the SAT test at 8:00 a.m.

After the homecoming game, he decided to hang out with friends. The next morning, he woke up, didn't ice his body, and didn't eat breakfast. He arrived early to the test site, showed his driver's license for ID, had three sharp #2 pencils, and said a quick prayer before the test began. A few minutes into the test, he felt fatigued and couldn't focus. Suddenly, his eyelids were heavy, and the words were beginning to blur.

He couldn't concentrate and pull his thoughts together no matter how hard he tried. Knowing the SAT penalizes students for blank answers, for each section, Ralph waited for the test proctor to say, "Two minutes left for this section of the test." To Ralph, that was code to start filling in random bubbles. He became so frustrated with not being able to focus, he filled in all the bubbles and took a nap until the test was over. While the SAT is not a pass or fail test, a high score was needed for scholarship money, and the opportunity for free money slipped right through his hands!

Later, a chance to redeem himself as a good test taker came as the senior class prepared for The Ohio Peace Office Training Academy (OPOTA) security test. He studied one hundred and thirty-five Security Performance Objectives for thirty minutes, then took a break for thirty minutes, then resumed. Taking breaks helped avoid information overload and lack of focus. Rather than trying to memorize questions and answers, he learned definitions for the words pertained to the choices for the questions. Then, he practiced searching for key words in the questions, igniting a recognition of the material leading to the multiple-choice answers.

Next, he timed himself during the practice exams and took the approach of "I know it," or "I don't know it." This was used as a mental note to not stress out during the test if confused on a question. When it was time to take the real test, he was ready. Mentally, Ralph had laser-like focus on the task at hand, which proved to him that he had the ability to prepare and conquer tests. As the students entered the room with pencils in hand to take this multiple-choice test, Ralph smiled, glanced around the room, and said to himself, "I am number one. I will get the highest score on this test, and I will be the first one finished with this test."

The test proctor announced, "You may begin." For each question, Ralph looked for key words in the questions that aligned with the definitions of the multiple-choice answers. Within fifteen minutes, he had completed a one hundred and thirty-three question test. A few days later, Commander Copeland received the scores, and it was indeed true—Ralph had received the highest score in the class with a 95%.

This moment was bigger than any athletic victory he'd ever experienced. This was about preparation and learning how to take a test. This was a mental victory: he'd overcome test anxiety and the idea he could only get As writing papers. This accomplishment wrapped up the end of his senior year. There was only one more thing left to do—put on a cap and gown and wave to the crowd while crossing the stage at his high school graduation.

At graduation, Ralph was overwhelmed with feelings of accomplishment and relief. He remembered all the reasons why he hated school—waking up early in the morning to walk forty-five minutes to school and home in the rain, snow, and scorching heat. He remembered the terrible school lunches, the dress code, having many substitute teachers in sixth grade, and experiencing a teacher strike.

Then, he recalled how going against the grain helped keep him out of trouble. It helped him develop into the young man he wanted to be and not what others told him to be. Ralph was happy knowing he had completed high school, doing it his way. He dared to be positively different and figured out how to get a 3.0 despite his math and science shortcomings. In the end, it was the best of times with The Squad. Some of his close friends went away to different colleges across the country, some stayed home and went to college or trade schools, and others went to work full-time. The good thing is everybody was doing something positive.

After figuring out how to make it through grade school, it was now time to move away and figure out how to graduate from college.

A university is a human invention for the transmission of knowledge and culture from generation to generation, through the training of quick minds and pure hearts, and for this work no other human invention will suffice, not even trade and industrial schools.

\- Dr. W.E.B. Dubois

3

College Is More Than an Education—It's a Way of Life

WHO COULD SLEEP THE NIGHT BEFORE GOING TO COLLEGE? Well, Ralph couldn't. He was awake for twenty-four hours trying to imagine how to react or make decisions for "what if this happens" type of scenarios. He said to himself, "What if mom gets sick? How will I get home in case of an emergency? What about money for bills, and what about my brothers?" Many more questions rose throughout the night and over into the two-hour car ride to the University of Toledo.

His mind was on a two-hour non-stop Cedar Point roller coaster ride—the Top Thrill Dragster to be exact. His mind was racing with high hopes of success, reaching 420 feet while vertically accelerating at 120 mph, then dropping down to 0 at 130 mph with overwhelming thoughts of failure. He held a silent two-hour conversation with himself, posing the following questions while gazing out the window at the farmland on the highway:

Why am I the first person to go to college?

Is college really that hard?

How scary are the 200 and 500 people classes?

What if going to college isn't worth it?

What about my struggles in math and science—am I college material?

What if I graduate and I don't get a job?

Arriving to campus on a gloomy, rainy day with random lightning sightings and roaring thunder made matters worse for him psychologically. While rushing to gather his items in the rain from his friend's mom's van and into the dorm room, he noticed the overflowing loads of carts being transported past him by other students. His belongings totaled a few toiletries, a TV that needed a metal hanger for an antenna, two pair of gym sneakers, a duffle bag with one week of clothes, and a small, used refrigerator, whereas other students had brand-new Xboxes and PlayStation consoles, flat screen TVs, laptop and desktop computers, in addition to suitcases full of clothes.

The overall experience of getting acclimated to college life did nothing but resurge his hate for school even more!

Even worse, his roommate moved in the next morning, and it was déjà vu! Matt brought everything Ralph had seen in the hallways and more—a leopard rug, a futon, suitcases full of clothes, and a desktop computer. After a quick conversation acknowledging their common interest for sports, they talked about room etiquette and room cleaning, and exchanged numbers for emergency purposes.

Later, the clouds and rain disappeared, the sun shined bright, and campus came to life as the cookouts, bonfires, dancing exhibitions, and friendly chatter filled the campus with excitement. This relief would only last for the next 48 hours as classes began at 8:00 a.m. sharp Monday morning. Professors used the first week of classes to review the syllabus— which is considered a law contract between the student, professor, and the university—for each class. This document included the books needed for class. He registered for five classes and needed 12 books. The average cost was $100 per book; hence, he needed $1,200 for books the first term. Instead of panicking, he rented four books from the library, made friends with classmates, and shared five books. For other information, he relied on multiple college professor YouTube videos and national research websites.

Next, the syllabus covered assignments, tests, and classroom expectations. They discussed classroom etiquette: no talking while the professor is talking, cellphones are off, and laptops are for classroom learning purposes only. They were adamant about the expectation for their attendance and participation policies. Some professors took attendance while others did not, but all professors made it clear students should be speaking in class about the book readings or current events relevant to the course during each session for class participation points. Right from the start, it was clear to Ralph that over the next four years he should never miss the first day of classes—it's the most important day for each term!

Most importantly, he discovered it takes a few weeks to ease the transition into college for first-time students. Eventually, he received funds from financial aid and some family members to buy more books and clothes. Then, he realized the food at college was delicious—three meals a day in various locations, fast food restaurants on campus, and events with free pizza or burgers being served weekly. He took part in Monday night football social events, in addition to playing in NBA 2K, Call of Duty, and Madden video game tournaments. However, most of the time he could be found in the recreation center. This place was an athlete's playground. It had seven basketball courts, large weight rooms, and Olympic diving board swimming pools.

Although he was settling in just fine socially, academically was a different story. He was struggling to wake up at 7:00 a.m. on Tuesday and Thursday mornings to catch the bus to a different campus—Scott Park—for an 8:00 a.m. criminal justice class. Besides missing classes, his mathematic deficiencies started to resurface in his Mathematics for the Liberal Arts course. To Ralph, college math was a foreign language; he didn't understand it at all!

Later, the anxiety of receiving bad grades after the first submission of all course assignments loomed over his head. To ease the mental tension of stress, he unknowingly played basketball for five hours one night. Before he knew it, 8:00 p.m. had arrived, and all the cafeterias on campus were closed. Even worse, he had no money. Ralph was starving, and this night, sleeping for dinner was not going to work.

He was forced to do something he hadn't considered doing since arriving to college—call Kevin Coburn. They were introduced back in July at a neighbor's family gathering. He gave Ralph his number and told him to give him a call if he ever needed anything, but pride almost prevented him from calling. Ralph had been self-sufficient, self-reliant, and self-motivated to make it in college on his own. Besides, Kevin was a stranger, and the thought of having to owe this man anything later was pricking away at his skin.

While sitting on the elevated bed in his dorm room, he decided to give it a try. As the phone rang, he became more and more tense and frustrated at the fact he'd played basketball all day and forgotten to eat! *If he jokes with me for hooping all day and not eating, I'm hanging up and never calling again*, he thought. Luckily, he answered.

"Hello, is this Kevin?"

"Yes, what's going on?"

"This is Ralph, the young guy from the summer BBQ."

"Yes, I remember you. I've been waiting on you to call me."

It was getting late, and Ralph was extremely nervous with what he was about to ask next, but with a humbled tone, he said, "Man, my bad for calling if it's too late, but I don't have any money and all the cafeterias closed on me. Do you think you can help me out tonight?"

Without hesitation, Kevin replied, "I'll be there in twenty minutes, and I'll call you when I get on campus." Immediately after hanging up, Ralph got dressed. Within twenty minutes, he received a phone call and directed Kevin to his dorm. From there, they headed to a nearby restaurant.

They ate and exchanged personal life stories for hours. At this time, they both discovered their lives mirrored each other's: growing up the in same neighborhood, early trials and tribulations with family, athletic goals, and life goals. At the time, Kevin shared that he graduated from the university and was now a co-founder of an organization giving housing and holistic development to foster care kids in Toledo. Even more, he was personally committed to empowering young people and guiding them on a path to success using education as a tool.

"What's the big deal about college? Why is it so important, Kevin?"

"Your degree is a key. The worst thing you can do is drop out of college and not get your degree. It opens doors that can't be opened without it. If you listen and do 75% of the things I'm telling you, you'll be successful."

"What do you mean?"

"You got a girlfriend—don't get her pregnant until you finish college. Marriage is another thing. Right now, just don't have any babies."

Ralph nodded his head in agreement as Kevin continued.

"Next, whatever you do, don't stop going to class, don't get caught up in the party hype, but enjoy yourself. If you're partying more than studying, you won't last long."

At this moment, Kevin was no longer a stranger—he became Ralph's life optician. Kevin illustrated hope and a pathway to success. He showed Ralph a college degree means opportunities for people to live a quality lifestyle and help family. After noticing they had been sitting for hours with no more food, Kevin closed the tab and they headed out the door. But before Kevin drove Ralph back to campus, he said, "I have to show you something really quick while we're out this way."

Ten minutes down the road, Kevin pointed to his left and right saying, "You see that house right there? That's a $250,000 home with six bedrooms. A chemical engineer lives there. That brick house next to it, I believe, is about $300,000. That's my homeboy's house. He's a lawyer and his wife is an accountant. Marble floors, decked-out basement—it's a really nice house."

A puzzled look came across Ralph's face. He didn't want to ask a dumb question, but he couldn't help it. "Wait a minute, so regular people with degrees live in these mansions, not athletes? And they drive new cars—Mercedes, BMWs, and Cadillacs? How is that possible? These houses look like they were built for the rich and famous!"

The truck came to a stop, and Kevin gathered himself for what he was about to say next. "Indeed, regular people with college degrees live in these houses and drive new cars because they took care of business and completed their studies at different universities. Now, they can afford to live and drive comfortably. Remember, when you get to this point in life, it's about seeing where your money is going. A college degree opens up doors. The more degrees you have, in some cases, presents more opportunities to earn more money. Now, let's get out of the truck for a minute."

They were in a new housing development neighborhood minutes from campus. There was nothing but dirt on the ground and lumbers of wood stacked inside beginning phases of housing construction.

"You're standing in the living room of a house me and my wife are building. This is going to be an 18-foot ceiling, the bedroom has a walk-in closet, a full-basement, and our girls' rooms will be up top. We should be all moved in and settled by March or April. When it's finished, if you're interested, I'll bring you out here for a weekend."

Ralph was all in, "Yes, I'm up for it." After that, Ralph didn't say another word, he just took it all in. This was the connection he needed to get on track. If a college degree was this powerful, he couldn't wait to graduate! On the way back to campus, he reflected continuously on what he had seen and heard. Before he could exit the vehicle and head up to get ready for the rest of the week, Kevin emphasized statements he'd made early that evening.

"Don't hesitate to call me if you need anything. Don't get a girl pregnant, don't drop out of school, and make your top priority your degree. If you listen to 75% of what I tell you, you'll be successful."

To Ralph, 75% was a C grade, and he was smarter than that. He wondered what would happen if he listened to 100%. While preparing for classes the next day, he took a moment to self-reflect by looking at the stars. In that moment, it clicked—time was the greatest asset for learning how to navigate the college experience the first year, and he was failing at it miserably. It was clear based on the fact that Kevin had to take him to dinner after the cafeteria closed.

Weekly Schedule. Exhibit 2

	Sunday	Monday	Tuesday	Wednesday	Thursday	Friday	Saturday
7:00 AM	Free time	Free time		Free time		Free time	Free time
8:00 AM			CRIM 1040 8 am - 9:30 am		CRIM 1040 8 am - 9:30 am		
9:00 AM							
10:00 AM							
11:00 AM			Free time		Free time		
12:00 PM							
1:00 PM							
2:00 PM		ENGL 1100 2 pm - 3:45 pm		ENGL 1100 2 pm - 3:45 pm			
3:00 PM							
4:00 PM		Lunch					
5:00 PM		CRIM 1010 5 pm- 9 pm	Math 1180 5 pm - 6:45 pm		Math 1180 5 pm - 6:45 pm		
6:00 PM							
7:00 PM							
8:00 PM				Free time			
9:00 PM		Free time	Free time		Free time		
10:00 PM							
11:00 PM							
12:00 AM							

This is an example of Ralph's weekly schedule the first two months of college. It shows the days and times of class and the free time afforded to students outside the classroom.

After reviewing his weekly schedule, it was even more clear he was doing too much of nothing, and it showed as the first assignment grades were sent out that week. He received papers back in classes that should have been sure As, but he received Cs and a lot of red ink. At best, he assumed graded math assignments would be Cs, but they were big red Fs. This was a major reality-check moment. Failing out of school was something he could *not* afford to do.

Ralph had four classes totaling fifteen credit hours, making him a full-time student. The schedule above shows the days and times of the courses, but most importantly, it shows how much free time he had outside of class. This free time included recreational basketball, video games, parties, or lounging with his girlfriend. It didn't include a job, studying, or even committing adequate time for class assignments.

Ralph conceded that, during his first month of college, he was mentally lost and in outer space, sailing through the galaxy. The fast life of college had gotten to him. The freedom was exhilarating. The first few weeks were wild, there were no real rules—or so he thought at the moment— the campus experience was reality TV minus the cameras.

There were distractions everywhere: girls, parties, alcohol, drugs, and sex. Then there were the athletic events, free food events on campus, the guest speakers, the talent shows, and more. Even more, it was the vast number of friends and hang-out places that grew daily. Not to mention, the six degrees of separation—everybody knew everybody, either from playing basketball, video game tournaments, or just connecting with people at party events.

Rather than panic about his grades, he made swift changes to his schedule that included a job and studying. There were plenty of jobs on campus: working in the cafeteria, fast food restaurants, custodial work, and work-study jobs in campus offices. From his award letter—financial aid— he qualified for work-study, which totaled up to $5,000 for the year, $2,500 per semester. After searching the career board in the Student Union, he found a work-study job at the testing center at the Scott Park campus.

Next, he went to the library and asked for help finding a math tutor who was available on Tuesday and Thursday evenings. He chose evening tutor sessions over the morning sessions because going to see the tutors right after class to review notes and ask specific questions while the information was fresh aided his ability to understand various math equations better.

After a few sessions, he made appointments to meet with the same math tutor two times a week for one-hour sessions. After the math tutoring, he moved to the fourth floor, using one of the quiet library rooms to complete writing assignments for English and criminal justice courses. If there wasn't an assignment to complete, he would read five to ten pages from various criminal justice course textbooks or watch professor lectures on YouTube.

Next, after learning how to increase study time, he focused on managing time for parties. As college freshman, the freedom to live a rock star lifestyle overtakes the minds of students; therefore, a reality check was needed in order to slow down. If not, the likelihood of failing or dropping out of college increases within the first two weeks of the first semester for freshman students.

Also, taking control of party time was important to minimize the probability of being involved in dangerous activities. For college students, this included underage alcohol consumption, unprotected sex, drug abuse, or a violent act against another person rather on or off campus, resulting in college expulsion. A student's personal record is priceless after college because employers do background checks prior to hiring, and the smallest violation or sanction could decide if the job is offered or taken away.

As the semester progressed, he became an introverted extrovert. Although he liked being around people and enjoyed the adventures, there were times he'd much rather be alone. He found peace of mind going to breakfast, lunch, or dinner alone, going to the gym and working out alone, shooting hoops alone, playing video games alone, and sometimes just sitting down and collecting his thoughts alone. After a few weeks of getting the hang of college life, he put together the following schedule for the rest of the fall semester. This schedule would be the foundation for time management over the next four years.

Time Management Schedule. Exhibit 3

	Sunday	Monday	Tuesday	Wednesday	Thursday	Friday	Saturday
7:00 AM	Peace of Mind Time	Morning Prep	Morning Prep	Morning Prep	Morning Prep	Open	Open
8:00 AM			CRIM 1040 8 am - 10:30 am		CRIM 1040 8 am - 10:30 am		
9:00 AM		Work Study Job 9 am - 2 pm		Work Study Job 9 am - 2 pm			
10:00 AM							
11:00 AM			Work Study Job 11 am - 3pm		Work Study Job 11 am - 3 pm		
12:00 PM							
1:00 PM							
2:00 PM		ENGL 1100 2 pm - 3:45 pm		ENGL 1100 2 pm - 3:45 pm			
3:00 PM							
4:00 PM	Friend Time	Lunch	Lunch	Lunch	Lunch		
5:00 PM		CRIM 1010 5 pm- 9 pm	Math 1180 5 pm - 6:45 pm	Gym Time	Math 1180 5 pm - 6:45 pm		
6:00 PM							
7:00 PM	Girl friend Time		Math Tutor		Math Tutor		
8:00 PM							
9:00 PM	Dorm Room	Dorm Room	Library Study	Dorm Room	Library Study		
10:00 PM							
11:00 PM			Dorm Room		Dorm Room		
12:00 AM							

This is Ralph's revised schedule. It shows a better use of time as a college student. He used this template to figure out how to better use time over the next four years of college.

By the time he figured out the cadence for learning to live on his own, the semester was coming to an end, and the holiday season was approaching, meaning the spring course registration portal was open. He reviewed the degree audit. It details how many classes and what classes a student needs to take to graduate in four years. Then, he went online and began scheduling classes according to the schedule he had created for the fall semester, except this time, he refused to take any class before 10:00 a.m. The other important part was ensuring a full schedule of fifteen credit hours and no classes on Friday. Having a three-day weekend was awesome!

A moment of clarity presented itself at this time. He reflected on the highs and lows of the first semester of college. College is more than learning in the classroom, it's learning how to live, socialize and be academically successful at the same time. This is important to balance the college culture. A significant part of college was preparing for tests called *finals*. Remembering the experience, he had failing the SAT test in high school, he changed his approach this time. He went to sleep early the entire week, woke up and ate breakfast, and arrived at all his classes twenty minutes early.

Arriving early gave him a little more time for last-minute studying. At the end of the week, he was happy it was over, but wasn't confident in his results given the rough start to the semester. Nonetheless, with finals in the books and the academic advisor confirming the courses selected for the spring semester, momentum was building. There was only a moment to spare to take a break for Christmas—then, he was right back to college.

The holiday celebrations passed, grades were posted, and a sense of relief overwhelmed Ralph as he struggled to acclimate to the college culture. He finished the first semester with a 2.3 grade point average, the hardest C average he'd ever managed in his academic career. Nevertheless, he reflected again on the semester and counted more good than bad outcomes. First, going to the math tutor helped him get a C and was well worth the time. Next, he had always been an exceptional writer, but the other grades he received in writing-dominant courses didn't equate, more so because he didn't put forth the time needed to submit quality work at the beginning of the year. However, the spring semester was coming up and with it, an opportunity to redeem himself academically. It was all he could think about.

WITH THE SPRING SEMESTER underway, he strutted around campus, more comfortable, more assertive, and more knowledgeable of how to navigate the university landscape. He knew where the financial aid office was located, tutoring labs, Trio centers, and study room were located. Even more, his ability to build friendships with other students continued. From the start, he assessed the new class schedule, figured in 20 hours for work study, time for library studying, and instead of working with a math tutor, he began working with writing coaches to increase his ability to write essays and reports. In Northern Ohio, the spring semester started off colder; therefore, it was easier to skip parties at the beginning of term because everyone on campus focused on staying warm until March.

After two good months of studying and gaining a clearer understanding of college, Ralph was ready to give an update on his progress and check in with Kevin. The timing was perfect—Kevin and his family moved into the new house and invited Ralph over. It was a beautiful house with three floors, five bedrooms, granite countertops, an eighteen-foot living room ceiling, a two-car garage, and a plethora of land in the backyard—exactly how he said it would look. This was the dream, to get a house like this after college.

It was a good weekend filled with encouragement and positive energy, helping Ralph finish the spring semester strong. He studied, completed assignments, watched his partying, kept good health by working out in the gym, saved some money, completed the financial aid application again, and registered for fall classes. As the spring term ended, he had the hardest time mentally going home for the summer. His first year of college was a whirlwind, but he adapted and figured it out.

Back home, it was clear to everyone he was different, in a good but awkward way. He was still cool, but all he talked about was what happened the first year of college. It was as if he was obsessed with it. He shared his dreams and told his friends about some of the people he had met and how he had overcome some of life's trials and tribulations while away. He talked about buying homes, having nice cars, and dressing in better clothes after college. He also talked about taking trips to Houston, Atlanta, Las Vegas, Miami, and even Africa in the upcoming years, for he knew a college degree would change his life forever.

Sadly, while trying to convince friends, he recognized a disconnect. Annoyed by his consistent chatter of college, one person abruptly said,

"You still talking about college? You do know you have to pay the loans back, with interest? You're paying it back, right?"

"Yes, I know, but I have it figured out. At best, I might owe $70,000 in loans, and when I graduate, I'll make between $30,000 and $40,000 to start.

"Man, you're dreaming. No jobs around here are gonna pay you that much money!"

"Yes, they will, and even more later, after I get some years of experience."

Rather than be quiet, Ralph felt an obligation to share what he had learned with his friends who were unaware of the possibilities of success resulting from attending college. It wasn't that he thought he was better than anybody; it was the fact he had been exposed to different things. Therefore, his mind had evolved past the present and into the future.

"Wait a minute, let me paint this picture for you. My salary could rise well above $60,000 by the time I'm 30 years old. So, the math say's I'll make about $500,000 in 10 years."

"But what about the loans, Ralph?"

"If I don't go living above my means, I could pay $100,000 after interest in loans back and will have made $400,000."

"Sounds good, but I thought you weren't that good in math," said another.

Ralph smirked. "I've always been good at counting money."

From experience, he knew success in college is attributed to having a steady cash flow. Therefore, he put his OPOTA certificate to use and got a job working security at Progressive Field, the Cleveland Indians' ball park stadium. Working nights and days there helped time pass over the summer. Daily, he wondered about the upcoming year, still posing the same questions he did on the first day he arrived at the university. He remembered graduating from high school was mandatory but graduating from college was a privilege. After what he learned the first year, there was no doubt getting a degree would provide the best means of creating a positive life for himself and his family.

THIS TIME AROUND WAS DIFFERENT. There was a sense of relief going into the second year. The fear of the unknown disappeared.

Ralph and his buddies from his first year moved into one of the new dorms. This dorm was built suite style, comfortably rooming four people per unit. It had two rooms with two beds in each—four beds total—that were separated by a big mirror in the middle. There was also a sink in the living room separating the toilet from the stand-up shower room. In addition, the living room space in the dorm provided access to free wi-fi, a room phone line, and cable connection for the TV.

While the amenities were nice, rooming on campus for the second year with guys that Ralph considered family was everything! If one person ate, everybody ate. If somebody needed a ride, transportation was available. If somebody needed clothes, shoes, or some nights, a place to sleep—it was given. Literally, the second year took off like a rocket!

He was familiar with the sequence of events that occurred on the college campus since he attended them all last year, but most importantly, knowing how college professors taught the courses eased learning tension. But during the first week of classes, he noticed the syllabuses from many of his professors were different. Rather than essay assignments, these professors chose to have weeks of lectures and class discussions and grades on two tests: a mid-term test and a final test. Another difference was he didn't need a lot of books for the lecture courses. The focus during this semester was learning information from the professors' abilities to breakdown PowerPoint presentations from a philosophical analysis of theory and applicable practices.

The first year was intimidating, but during the second year, Ralph learned how to catch the rhythm to be a part of class discussions, debates, and ideas to help grasp the information during courses. Being heard is a part of the learning experience. Some professors lecture—very long speeches—for two hours or more. For lectures, students must read ahead. If he didn't read at least one chapter before lectures, he would be lost in the maze of information shared by the professors.

Class participation during lecture courses is required and can be difficult for shy students. So, rather than speak during every discussion, he'd listen attentively then choose specific things that sparked interest. This strategy helped prompt him to speak more in the class sessions. This tactic was used his second year to gain recognition from professors, and it helped build positive relationships in and out of class.

While Ralph figured out how to navigate the classroom experience, it was life outside of college that would become a concern. For instance, *alcoholism* is a major problem in college. This form of intoxication often leads to *Drinking and Driving*. This type of poor decision making endangers the lives of everyone: passengers, drivers, and pedestrians. Equally, underage consumption of alcohol and operating a vehicle under the influence would ruin opportunities for career obtainment during and after college. For example, a fellow sophomore classmate, Claude, was arrested the second week of classes for underage consumption of alcohol and operating a vehicle while under the influence.

Claude had to rethink his future and dropped out of college to pursue another pathway to success. Claude's dream was to become a police officer, but he would not be hired because of his criminal record. Word spread around campus fast—students, faculty, and staff continuously reiterating the dangers—and in the end, Ralph decided it just wasn't worth it. No need to chance it.

Besides, Kevin called Ralph one afternoon in September, inviting him down to his office to discuss a job opportunity as a youth advocate for foster care kids working with The House of Emmanuel. This added motivation not to drink and drive, not to engage in underage consumption, and most importantly, not to get into any trouble on the college campus. In fact, this was the opportunity he needed to get work experience and make some more money. This job was centered around his current school and work-study schedule.

He created a routine that worked perfectly, and from there, navigating college became as easy as a walk in the park. He'd go to class, and from class, he'd go to the work-study job. At the work-study job, he read ten to fifteen pages at a time and completed class work. After the work-study job, he conducted school and home visits for foster care kids. Last, he attended a night class if there was one; if not, then it was time to meet friends at the gym. Since Ralph roomed with his friends, it was easier to keep a curfew because every day, someone would come to the dorm and play video games at night or watch sports events. Unfortunately, the routine he created slowly disappeared, and everything wasn't going as smoothly as it seemed.

Although it appeared Ralph was in control, he wasn't. In fact, the fall semester consumed Ralph so much that his studies plunged to the bottom of the Atlantic Ocean. Between working multiple jobs, social events, relationship activities, and social events with friends, course work was out of sight and out of mind.

A group of friends that moved into the off-campus apartments were throwing parties every night. Literally, every night! Plus, the "social media phenomenon" had taken over—it was pandemonium on campus. In fact, Ralph along with other students, rented laptops from the library just to have access to social media during class time. More than half the classes this term was filled with students using laptops to browse social media websites instead of taking notes.

Not to mention, Ralph had been focusing on making money more than getting his work done. On days he would usually go to the work-study job on campus, he would be out working with the foster care youth. The hours he was logging became so noticeable, one Friday when he went to the office to pick up his check, Kevin had some words to say.

"Good work! I see you're logging the contacts and the hours, and your reports on the youth are great. I noticed this is your biggest check so far, so you're putting in a lot of time working, but how are you doing with your studies?"

Ralph grinned and looked away, trying not to give Kevin any reason to be more suspicious, and said, "I'm doing great! Everything is cool. I'm not failing out, I'm still in school."

But there was a different flare about Ralph this year—it was as if he was on a money chase and was losing focus on school. Kevin was sure Ralph had become infatuated with buying new things and having freedom from the money he made.

From Ralph's perspective, college had become a convenient inconvenience. He was missing class to go to work. He figured changing lives and making money doing it was more impactful than sitting in the classroom. When he was in class, instead of paying attention to the lectures, he daydreamed about buying new clothes. Even worse, if he wasn't searching through social media outlets on the computer in the back of the class, he was writing notes about his finances for the month. This semester turned into being socially active and working and completing course work fell to the bottom of his priorities. It was clear, and Kevin could see it. He knew Ralph was losing focus on school, and knowing this, he redirected his attention to the main prize.

"Ok, cool. After this semester, do me a favor."

"I got you, whatever it is."

Kevin stared him down with a stern look and said, "Show me your report card when grades post at the end of the term."

Ralph shrugged and laughed, "Okay, will do."

During the drive back to campus, he reflected on his conversation with Kevin. The more he thought about it, the more it put Ralph in a panic. First, he thought about this term and how he'd lost focus, then he thought about the teachers he selected this term. They weren't essay driven professors—they were multiple-choice test type professors! This was bad, because he had overcommitted himself to obligations outside of college and forgotten about the importance of putting school above everything! After getting his mid-term grades back, it was clear this was a failed semester.

No matter how much he tried to catch up before finals, he just couldn't do it. He partied too much! Relaxed with his girlfriend too much! Went to the gym to shoot hoops too much! He also worked outside of the hours he dedicated to jobs too much!

Finals arrived faster than Superman flying past a locomotive. There wasn't enough time to catch up on all the information from the start of the term. It was the SAT test scenario all over again: he was severely underprepared. The difference between being underprepared for the SAT test and this time was that failing would cost thousands of dollars—one semester's worth was $10,000 to be exact! All the prayer in the world wouldn't prevent the lesson God was gearing to show Ralph this term. The grades posted the following week, and his heart dropped to the floor. He had a 1.56 grade point average for the fall term: four Ds and one B-.

He headed back home for Christmas Break, and there was only one thing on his mind—getting kicked out of school and losing financial aid support. He'd overheard stories from friends who struggled to get back in school after partying too hard freshman year. In some cases, students went a term or two paying tuition and fees out of pocket. Prior to getting reinstated, they had to prove they were serious about learning and pass the courses they paid for. At the end of the process, they'd have to fill out more paperwork to receive financial aid support again. Another route some students took was going to a community college for lower cost to pass similar courses then transferring back to the university with a proven record of scholastic achievement. While both are options to get back in, the goal is to never get kicked out!

In fact, financial aid will not fund tuition, fees, or room and board for a student who doesn't excel academically. Students must pass courses. In addition to possibly losing financial aid, Ralph dreaded the possibility of being humiliated by friends for having to go back to living in his mom's house. That alone pushed him to rethink and refocus on excelling academically.

Although the 1.56 grade point average was disgraceful, he did not get kicked out of school, but was instead placed on academic probation. He had to get above a 2.0 grade point average during the spring term or lose financial support. Therefore, when the spring semester started, his demeanor changed, he was focused on the task at hand. Even more, he needed to find enthusiasm for learning or he wouldn't last the next two years. He was over the dorm life, and quite frankly, he was over college. He just wanted to make money. This spring, he studied more and did better selecting teachers that taught to his strengths. But midway through the semester, he still had difficulties with becoming lackadaisical.

No matter how hard he tried to remain engaged in the classroom, it proved to be harder and harder by the day. Ralph desperately needed a mental boost to rededicate his focus on learning, and fast. With the sun beginning to shine and campus starting to come alive, it was just a matter of time before the motivation he sought after would be standing directly in front of him.

"We don't remember days, we remember moments."

- Cesare Pavese

4

Inspiration

THERE WAS SOMETHING DIFFERENT ABOUT CAMPUS MIDWAY THROUGH THE SEMESTER. All the commotion on campus was for a reason he didn't understand—people were excited about an NPHC (National Pan-Hellenic Council) step show. The senior students attending the university told him, "This is the first one on campus in years, that's why it's a big deal. You better get a ticket, or you'll be left at the front door. The Doermann Theatre is going to sell out." Ralph had never experienced a campus event like this. The energy was surreal, and it wasn't the homecoming football game, NCCA tournament basketball game, or a fall icebreaker party—it was a fraternity/sorority step show.

Because of the hype for this event, he invited his younger brother Deonte to campus the weekend of the show. He figured it was important for his brother to see this event, too, especially since the university he was playing basketball at didn't have an NPHC. This would be something they both could experience together since neither knew anything about Greek step shows, let alone fraternities and sororities. After getting dressed, Ralph and his brother nonchalantly walked through campus toward the theatre. As they got closer, they noticed more and more people were walking to the Doermann Theatre, too, except with tickets in their hands.

But as they approached, they noticed the pay-at-the door line was wrapped around the corner. After about ten minutes in line, they were third from the counter. Ralph had twenty dollars in his hand, prepared to get him and his brother a seat to see the show. As they approached the counter, the cashier closed the window, walked from behind the counter then out the door, announcing to the hundreds of people behind them, "Sorry, everyone! The theatre is sold out. Again, the theatre is sold out. No more tickets available!"

Upset about the announcement, some patrons exited the building in an uproar, while others skipped to the front of the line, trying their best to pay more money than needed for admission, but it didn't work. Ralph quietly moved his brother aside and stood by the door patiently, not losing hope for entry. He felt in his spirit there was a reason they shouldn't walk out the door with the raging crowd, but at the time he just didn't know why. A few seconds later, he looked up and slapped five to C.P. as he approached the counter. He was one of the many friends he had made his first year.

"Ralph, what's up? What are you doing out here?"

"They sold out of tickets, and nobody else is getting in. You might as well turn around."

C.P. looked around to see who was close and in a discreet manner said, "Word, I'm the emcee for the step show. You've never been to one, right? Hold on a for second, let me see what I can do." Ralph watched C.P. walk through the door, pulling a different lady from the back. He said, "I'm emceeing, and they told me I get two guests. Those two right there…" He pointed at Ralph and his brother. "… are with me. Can you get them in?" The lady replied, "Sure, it's just going to be hard for them to find seats, though."

As she opened the door, Ralph and his brother slid in quickly before the crowd could become irate and slapped five with C.P. one more time as a "thank you" gesture. Next, they walked into the theatre and noticed it was packed like a Michael Jackson concert, from wall to wall, and there wasn't a seat in sight, standing room only. Nonetheless, they were happy just to get in. Within seconds, C.P. was on stage, and the show was beginning.

In between the DJ playing party music and giving away prizes, C.P. called each group out one by one to strut their stuff. During this time, the crowd learned a little history about each NPHC organization participating in the step show. NPHC was also known as the "Divine 9," five fraternities for men and four sororities for women. The fraternities for men are Alpha Phi Alpha, Kappa Alpha Psi, Omega Psi Phi, Phi Beta Sigma, and Iota Phi Theta. The sororities for women are Alpha Kappa Alpha, Delta Sigma Theta, Zeta Phi Beta, and Sigma Gamma Rho. The ladies and gentlemen representing their respective organizations put on a show!

All the participants moved with grace, in unison and with precision. With every thundering step came a sound of purpose. They chanted their mottos, sung their songs, and exemplified a showmanship to be remembered. Every organization taking part was a winner in Ralph's eyes.

The courage, hard work, and dedication devoted to give a stellar performance on that big stage was remarkable. It was such an enjoyable time, no one wanted it to end, but Ralph was ready to do some homework and learn more about these organizations on his own. This moment motivated him to the next level of figuring out how to navigate through college—learn as much as possible about the organizations in the step show.

After the step show, his brother went back to the dorm while Ralph went to the library to research the "Divine 9" organizations. While there, he learned they were founded on college campuses focusing on scholarship, brotherhood and sisterhood bonds, and service projects uplifting the community. He further learned about a few notable members associated with these organizations and their monumental contributions to society: Toni Morrison and Katherine Johnson, Alpha Kappa Alpha; Shirley Chisholm and Dr. Nikki Giovanni, Delta Sigma Theta; Zora Neale Hurston and Sheryl Underwood, Zeta Phi Beta; Hattie McDaniel and Kelly Price, Sigma Gamma Rho; Jesse Owens and Thurgood Marshall, Alpha Phi Alpha; Johnny Cochran and Wilt Chamberlain, Kappa Alpha Psi; Michael Jordan and Dr. Charles Drew; Omega Psi Phi; Dr. George Washington

Carver and Emmitt Smith, Phi Beta Sigma; Spencer Christian and Terrence Carson, Iota Phi Theta.

The lists continued, naming leaders in entertainment, education, government, and athletics that joined one of the "Divine 9." But more so than thinking about joining a fraternity or sorority to participate in a step show, this moment showed him that for two years all he did was go to work, class, attend parties, and play basketball. This was a sad moment, given the vast number of opportunities to get involved and take part in positive movements and celebrations on campus.

By conducting more research and looking into the clubs and other organizations on campus funded by the college to put on events run by students, Ralph was inspired to get involved. Even better, he wanted to run for offices and become either President, Vice President, or Treasurer for an organization on campus. Contrarily, it was noted that in order to hold one of these positions, 2.5 to 3.0 GPAs are required depending on the organization. Now, he was rejuvenated and refocused on learning, something he desperately needed.

Although he managed not to party and work as much this semester, his attention was still low. With just a few weeks remaining, he recovered from the fall travesty to get a 2.5 GPA for the spring term, but he was still not ready to show Kevin his report card. As a matter of fact, every time Kevin mentioned it, he would create a story that slowly started with, "See what had happened was…" before quickly changing the subject.

But one particular time, he changed the subject to talk to Kevin about joining one of the fraternities, and he quickly replied, "I don't care if you join one or not, but remember, you came to college to graduate. You have two years left to get your degree—don't mess it up! Oh, and you need a high grade point average, among other things, to be considered for membership in a fraternity. But right now, you need to decide if you're going home for the summer or getting an apartment."

The decision to go home or stay in the city and get an apartment was a big deal. Living alone in the city is a different level of responsibility. It's more bills. Although living in a dorm seemed as if it was a lot of money, it's extremely beneficial from a cost of living perspective. Dorms provide security, electricity, internet, cable, basic furniture needs, and some have cafeterias, whereas apartments are truly only good for privacy.

Think about the expenses. In many cases, they outweigh the value of an apartment for college students after factoring in gas for the car, car insurance, car payments, campus parking, and grocery shopping. Then, paying for cable, internet, electric and gas bills, costs of furniture, and in many cases, expensive rent. Having an apartment seemed more inconvenient than being a help. So, he considered a single room on campus as an RA—a residential advisor—but missed the deadline to apply. Being an RA is a job overseeing a dorm floor. It comes with free room and board and meals for a year—this would've been clutch. Consequently, with options dwindling down and the one-free-month-rent summer apartment specials getting more and more enticing, a single apartment ten minutes away from campus was selected.

"BACK TO THE BASICS" WAS RALPH'S MINDSET GOING INTO FALL TERM JUNIOR YEAR. That meant getting back to doing what he did best: reading, writing, and going against the grain. This fall term, he was on a mission. By working with the academic advisor every semester, Ralph finally put together a schedule that would get him a 3.0 grade point average his junior year. The two classes he'd received Ds in were being retaken using grade deletions. Then, he scheduled an online class that could be taken at home on the computer. Next, he focused on taking part in clubs, organizations, and programs to help build a professional resume.

This year, he didn't participate in any of the back to school events. He wanted to minimize anything he considered to be a distraction and started going against the grain again. If everybody was going to a party, he'd stay home. While everybody was on social media, he'd stay away from it. There were times early in the year when some of his friends would call him a "stranger" when he was on campus. This was because nobody saw him at the house or club parties as much as they did last year.

Then, he transitioned from going against the grain to a winner's mentality of competing for first place in the classroom. He showed up to all his classes first, sat in the first row, and greeted all his professors first! Sitting in the first row was his way to ensure attentiveness by not sitting in the back of the class browsing social media. This was also a way to be recognized more because the professors typically called on students in the first row for participation points.

When it was time to discuss the syllabus, he was familiar with the expectations, assignment structure, and test protocols. He even knew the professors used information in books from prior courses, so he didn't sell his books back to the university at the end of the last spring term. By doing this, he was already ten steps ahead of everyone else. In addition, he continued to study by watching other professor's YouTube channels—he used this method to have more conversations about the course work assignments and readings with fellow classmates. Altogether, it was easier to recall knowledge shared from conversations and some YouTube channels alongside the information shared in textbooks.

It took him three years to get it, but he finally caught the cadence of college and was more confident than he'd ever been. He was able to keep up with the pace of learning academically and socially. So, for the fall semester, he focused on networking. While he had built a great network of guys, he lacked a network of women. *This wouldn't be hard*, he thought, especially since women outnumbered the men everywhere but the basketball courts in the recreation center on campus.

There were more women professors, students, and more women in other roles on campus than men. There were even more women taking part in organization events on campus. They were beautiful! But beyond their beauty, he saw the intelligence they showed on the college campus and thought about the women in the world. He figured if the women on campus were beautiful, the women in the workplace must be gorgeous. Therefore, it would be best to learn how to build and sustain healthy, respectful relationships with the opposite sex as early as possible. Failure to do so could create unfortunate circumstances that could affect his life disastrously later: sexual harassment lawsuits, disrespectful gender bias comments resulting in firing, and other detrimental behaviors impacting man-woman relationships in the workplace.

Rather than complimenting the ladies on their looks or bodily figures, he'd rather talk about dream jobs, next steps after college, graduate school, internship opportunities, or job fairs. These conversations would take place in the cafeteria, at student events, or sometimes before class started in the hallways. Usually, after a common interest was found, an exchange of phone numbers or email information would follow. This would be noted as a business contact for safe keeping for the future.

College presents the best opportunity to skillfully prepare for the future by forging bonds that would become professional networks after graduation: nurses, engineers, doctors, lawyers, entrepreneurs, accountants, computer programmers, and teachers. These positive relationships would be impactful for information sharing after college and to help one another if a time of need should come. As he became more comfortable developing professional relationship networks with the ladies on campus, other opportunities arose. He began networking with everybody: Caucasian, African-American, Hispanic, Asian, African. Ethnicity or gender didn't matter. Ralph would've bet his last dollar that whoever he crossed paths with was going to be successful in the future. And the people whose numbers he didn't get, he connected with on social media. While making friends on social media, he began reevaluating his image, reviewing pictures, status post comments, and even random friends he'd accepted requests from.

Social media images were highly important as Ralph worked with professors to secure an independent study for the spring and an internship for the summer. These opportunities were not handed out to everyone— they were earned over the years, and he didn't want to mess things up. He removed party images, and although he was twenty-one years old at the time, professors constantly reiterated that pictures eluding to alcohol abuse or belligerent intoxications would not be positively received by future employers.

"So much depends on reputation—guard it with your life."

- Robert Greene

While it may seem as if Ralph might have gotten off track his junior year, he did not. He focused on other things that made him a well-rounded student. By putting together a comfortable work schedule, participating in student organization events, and understanding how professors taught, he finally figured out school at the next level. The best part was that he didn't give up. Although the learning cadence was hard for a moment going into finals week, he was genuinely excited for the first time in the last three years.

But even more, at the end of the term, he was finally prepared to show Kevin his report card. He smiled, then frowned.

"The 3.0 is great, but what about these other terms? And was this 1.5 when you were working with me? Had I seen this earlier, you would have been fired."

Ralph laughed and shrugged. "Of course not."

Nonetheless, a more pressing concern now was how to prepare for internships. These opportunities were unpaid, but students received college credits. Kevin emphasized important points of professionalism: wearing ties, punctuality, assertiveness, and most importantly as a student, being there to absorb the knowledge and learn. The spring semester independent study was something that had to be earned and sought after. Ralph approached his professors about the opportunity in the fall, and because of his persistence and scholar reputation in the classroom, he earned the opportunity to serve as an offender reentry liaison for the criminal justice department at the college.

This learning experience happened in the community at various locations twice a month. The independent study required Ralph to attend community meetings, take notes, and write reports on how convicted felons were transitioning back into society after years in prison. At this time, he saw how offenders, law enforcement officers, nonprofit organization leaders, and employers led conversations on jobs, education opportunities, and parole restrictions hindering offenders' progress.

Over the next few weeks, an internship with the parole authority had been solidified for him to work 200 hours during the summer. He remembered what Kevin had said: "Everybody is watching." For this reason, he spent his summer doing two things: working at the internship from 8:00 a.m. – 4:00 p.m. and security from 6:00 p.m. – 12:00 a.m. Monday through Friday from June to August.

As he entered on the first day, he was introduced to all the parole officers in the office, then sat down with the supervising officer, Gabe, to review the terms of the internship. Gabe had been working in the criminal justice field for over ten years, starting out as a correction officer in the prison and later, transferring to parole when a job became available. His demeanor was professional all the way, and he reiterated continuously that paroles were convicted criminals, and their information was not to be shared or spoken about outside of the office. Ralph nodded in agreement saying, "Yes, I understand." Then, he was assigned to Larome Myrick.

The first thing Larome had Ralph do when he started was complete a job application to become a correction officer. Although Ralph refused to do it at first, thinking it was pointless, he listened and did it anyway. In his mind, he thought it wouldn't matter, because a parole officer job would be available at the end of graduation anyway. Nevertheless, after he finished the application, he shadowed Larome and his field partner, Dave, completing field work and home and job visits to ensure parole compliance, but during home visits, he stayed in the car for safety reasons.

Moreover, Ralph sat in briefing meetings, helped complete new parole paperwork, and went over to the jail daily to learn how to release offenders. He paid attention to every detail and listened to every professional he met throughout the internship. This was the experience he needed. Every day, he kept a journal of things he did to help strengthen his resume to apply for positions after graduation. As the summer months flew by, over 200 internship hours were completed. The only thing to do now was finish the remaining courses the following year and graduate.

Consequently, shocking news would put a major barrier in front of Ralph, causing him to make decisions that would change his life forever!

"You may encounter many defeats, but you must not be defeated. In fact, it may be necessary to encounter the defeats, so you can know who you are, what you can rise from, how you can still come out of it."

- Maya Angelou

5

Weathering the Storm

NO, THIS CAN'T BE TRUE! GRADUATION IS MONTHS AWAY! This wasn't the news Ralph was hoping for when he received a phone call from Larome at the start of fall term his senior year.

"Wait, say it one more time. You lost me, what's happening with the state, Larome?"

"A notice was sent out today. The state budget is being cut, and a hiring freeze is being placed on parole officer hiring next year. You might want to really consider the correction officer route. They'll call you soon, you just have to pass the state test and wait for a position to open."

"What's the deal with the state budget? I thought everything was working out fine."

"People aren't retiring from jobs at the rate they thought they would."

When he hung up the phone, his level of stress heightened, and his mind erupted like a volcano, overflowing with thoughts for back up plans to back up plans. Taking a job in another state was always a possibility, but he hadn't prepared for it. His current budget couldn't afford the cost to fly for the interview, hotels, gas, and other expenses for moving. This was something that should've been planned from the moment college started or before moving into the apartment. Although other parole officer jobs were available across the country, he just wasn't mentally prepared to make a leap that big at the time. On the other hand, working in the prison for two years was a choice worth exploring, but honestly, it was his last resort.

A few weeks later, as a possibility, Ralph took the correction officer test and passed it but was not enthused at the thought of working in a prison. He sought assistance from the career service center to map out different possibilities or other interests. DEA, FBI, and CIA came about, but his accumulative grade point average was not a 3.0 or higher; therefore, those options wouldn't work, and there were no exceptions made for federal hiring criteria. Then, he thought about college from another perspective: is it better to stay in school one more year to figure it out or graduate now not knowing what to do with the degree?

Along the trail to figuring this out, one person asked, "What have you done for community service?"

Bingo! A light came on. Around this time, Ralph joined one of the fraternities he had researched from the step show. He took part in two impactful national initiatives: "Go to High School, Go to College" and "A Voteless People is a Hopeless People." By taking leads on community initiatives, he was informed of positions within nonprofit organizations looking to hire students directly out of college with community involvement experience. The best part of being hired by these organizations was that the major of the bachelor's degree usually didn't matter.

Rather than rush the process at twenty-two years old, he figured one more year of college would be enough time for him to make a substantial impact on the community as well as build a stronger resume for careers outside of law enforcement. Every day, he searched for jobs and reviewed related skills and experience qualifications to ensure he met the least criteria based on his own college experience. If there was a criterion he didn't meet, he sought after opportunities in the community to fill the void by volunteering time with nonprofit organizations. For example, he helped with social media campaigns for marketing experience, talked to students about programs for recruitment, and put together power point presentations to enhance his public speaking skills. For financial experience, he worked on fundraising campaigns and small campus projects that included budgets of $500-$2,000.

Going into his fifth year, he repeated the same steps that got him the 3.0 grade point average and focused on community involvement. At the same time, he maintained a comfortable school and work schedule. This made for two solid years of experience that would be notable outside of the criminal justice field. As the fall semester ended, he was more comfortable and financially prepared to apply for criminal justice jobs and nonprofit organization positions all over the country. He had taken a year to save money, research living arrangements in different states, and check the salary range for positions in different areas.

Now, the main thing Ralph needed was an advantage. After completing documents for graduation in May, he began applying for jobs in April. Ralph applied to jobs early because at the end of the spring semester, thousands of students across the United States would be graduating and applying for similar jobs, too, and some would have better grade point averages and more experience than he might have. At this moment, he was simply guessing the odds of competition for certain jobs by planning ahead.

After learning about state budget cuts and layoffs, he realized a college degree doesn't mandate that you'll be handed a job after graduation, but it does enhance a person's ability to compete for the career of their choice. While applying to jobs, he let his professional network know and asked for advice. His network shared insight on how to apply for certain jobs, interviewing criteria, and how to negotiate starting salary ranges.

Amid preparing for the next phase in life, time passed in the blink of an eye. Ralph's last semester in college had come to an end. The final test was completed, the last essays were turned in, and a "thank you" to everyone who had believed in him and helped along the way was said. He spent the last five days partying like there was no tomorrow! The people he started college with were preparing to walk across the stage, too! The same ones who ate together, took care of one another, and protected each other! It was a wonderful feeling—the moment had finally arrived.

The university graduation ceremony was massive. Thousands of people were seated inside, and thousands more were outside in the parking lot, waiting to take victory pictures with students when it was over. This was a different type of feeling: it was a moment of peace, a moment of accomplishment, and most importantly, a moment of not falling to defeat, but figuring out how to win against all odds. It was at this time he gazed into the sea of excited, cheering supporters and reflected on how he had weathered the storm.

While standing in line waiting for his name to be called to walk across the stage, he flashed back to staying up twenty-four hours, wondering if he was college material. Even more, he vividly remembered the gloomy, rainy day arriving to campus. Now, on his graduation day, the sun was shining brightly. Ralph relived the moments of uncertainty, moving his belongings into the dorm in the rain. Then, he smiled at the time he called Kevin because he was starving, and how that night had changed his life forever.

Then, he acknowledged that the most important asset a college student can have is learning how to manage time. He recalled failing courses for not studying due to overworking and partying. Next, it was the moment C.P. helped him get into the step show on campus, reinvigorating his attention to college.

He also knew the lessons he had learned from professors who taught at a pace he could understand were a major part of his college success. Even more, the mentors and champions he had met throughout his college experience, positively helping him through his trials and tribulations as young adult, would always be noted. Then, there was the independent study, internship, and community service experiences that influenced how he saw the world beyond the classroom in addition to helping him be competitive in the job market.

Last, it was the positive influences within the fraternity that gave him the final push to make it across the finish line. And as he got closer to the stage, he handed the reader his name card, Ralph F. Murphy II, and was announced to the world as a college graduate. Family, friends, and others continued to cheer for him and his peers alike. As he looked around the graduation ceremony, he smiled even bigger—the positive connections he made and networks he built were with students walking across the stage, too! These connections were gearing up to enter the workforce as the next wave of doctors, lawyers, engineers, computer programmers, teachers, healthcare administrators and nurses, just like he believed they would!

After the ceremony, the pictures, dinners, and graduation parties solidified the end of a journey that had once seemed impossible to complete. When the celebrations ended, he took a deep breath and a sigh of relief, knowing this moment would only last for a short second.

While a career in criminal justice didn't come to fruition, a well-rounded approach to the college experience provided him with unlimited possibilities after graduating with a bachelor's degree. In fact, years later, he used the early life lessons and experiences shared to obtain a master's degree in leadership while working as college advisor in local high schools.

After years of working in high schools Ralph transitioned to careers within higher education helping student through college. The positive impact and influences he made at different colleges and universities opened a pathway to complete a doctorate degree in education.

Today, Ralph uses the experiences within this text, alongside the research conducted in the next chapter, to help thousands of students every year figure out school too!

"What we need in education is a much better understanding of students and learning from a motivational perspective, from a psychological perspective..."

- *Angela Lee Duckworth*

6

The Formula

$$(P)\ E^n\ x\ M\ \frac{Y}{D} + A - S = \underline{\hspace{2cm}}$$

IT'S YOUR TURN! The author discovered a hidden story within the order of operations in the equation above to show students how to figure out school for themselves. For decades, the author has painted pictures with words using the following concepts to help learners grasp and implement skills to be successful at every level of education. This information can be used by teachers, professors, parents, and community organizers to aid students from a motivational and psychological perspective while matriculating through the school system.

For all to learn how to navigate through school, one must answer the equation above on their own by following the order of operations—

parenthesis, exponents, multiplication, division, addition, and subtraction—

using the following concepts: *(P)* for **Pace**; E^n for **Exposure;** $\dfrac{Y}{D}$ for

Destiny; + A for **Accountability**; **- S** for **Strategy.** By following the rules

for mathematical equations using words instead of numbers, at the end, you

too will learn how to figure out school. It all begins with parentheses—*(P)*;

Pace.

(P) is **Pace**. For this concept, please know this is not the infamous

"hare vs. tortoise race," because speed is irrelevant in this equation. In the

culture of learning, pace is the cadence, or rhythm, of knowledge that

learners are mesmerized by according to Kenneth Rice in *The Pied Piper*

Effect. In this regard, the rhythm of learning can have a mesmerizing effect

on the attention span of students when they learn how to focus on a learning

symbol: words, numbers, computers, visual art, anatomy, chemical

elements, among other things.

As students grow, learn, and transition through the system, it is

imperative their energy is transmitted toward learning symbols that can

absorb their educational energy output to discover their learning pace. For example, Bill Gates, co-founder of Microsoft, discovered his pace in the eighth grade in the 1960s. Gates's learning symbol was an ASR-33 teletype: a computer. Learning how to write codes for computer programming systems became Gates's obsession. He admitted to skipping athletics to log more than 2,000 hours learning how to program computers from eighth grade until his senior year of high school. The valuable lesson here is Gates's fortune and global accolades are attributed to the learning foundations set up in his K-12 experience. From here, he attended Harvard University and continued to learn how to program computers.

Whereas Bill Gates discovered his pace with computers, another notable example is Katherine Johnson (*Hidden Figures*), NASA Mathematician. She focused on numbers. She counted everything from steps to dishes to silverware as a youth. In her early years, Katherine became so advanced in mathematical studies, she skipped grades.

Remarkably, she was in high school by the age of 13. This was largely because of her brilliance with calculating numbers. Her brilliance was further perfected as a student at West Virginia State College, now known as West Virginia State University.

Also, remember in the narrative, Ralph described discovering his pace through focusing on words. Words became life as Ralph wrote poems, raps, songs, and stories during sixth grade. At the same time, he read novels and biographies regularly. Later, his affinity for reading and writing would help him excel in life.

Overall, Bill, Katherine, and Ralph showed the ability to focus on a learning symbol of their choice. This helped them accelerate their learning skills. It's not what they did in the classroom, but where their minds traveled when school was over. For example, when the summer arrived, and school was out of session, do you believe Ralph stopped reading and writing, Bill stopped developing his programming skills, or Katherine stopped counting? They most certainly did not!

Knowing this, once a student learns their **Pace,** they'll transition to E^n which is **EXPOSURE**.

E^n **is Exposure.** Exposure creates energy from a vision to make it a reality. As a child evolves, their mind is formed by the things they see and hear. For this reason, increasing the amount of positive exposure is imperative while transitioning through school systems.

"But I was a child, you know, and when a child puts his eyes in the world, he has to use what he sees. There's nothing else to use. And you are formed by what you see, the choices you have to make…"

- James Baldwin

Ralph Emerson once said, "A man is what he thinks about all day long." Now couple Emerson's assertion with the quote noted above by Baldwin. Collectively, they illustrate that what a student sees early in life guides their thoughts into adulthood. Their mind is formed while exposed to things that increase their motivation; therefore, increasing the amount of positive exposure as they transition from high school to higher education institutions is highly important.

For this reason, it would help the learner to be open-minded toward everything that crosses their path. For Ralph, exposure was visiting colleges, career days, working with foster care kids, seeing large homes and nice cars, internships, and more.

"What you envision in your mind, how you see yourself, and how you envision the world around you is of great importance because those things become your focus."

- Dr. Eric Thomas, also known as "ET"

Shifting the way youths envision themselves is the most challenging aspect of today's education system. Now, to help shift the culture, the learning community must confront the "*Social Acceptance Bug*" plaguing the everyday lives of young people. The culture illustrates a "like me for who you think I am" but "not respect me for who I truly am" era. To be more specific, the *"Social Acceptance Bug"* means doing things to be liked.

A huge problem with school systems and social acceptance validation includes fashion. For example, hairstyles, clothes, shoes, make-up, or jewelry are becoming the focus, causing students to deviate their attention away from learning in the classroom. On another note, constant exposure to dreamy lifestyles are brainwashing students as they develop a "get to the money" mentality. This mentality erases delayed gratification, which is the patience to wait for the reward of taking the time for a post-secondary degree. It becomes easier to believe a nice car, nice home, and vacations are more attainable by picking up a basketball, singing, or modeling rather than learning how to program computers, exceeding expectations mathematically, making new scientific discoveries, or writing impactful stories.

In 2017, *"We Need More"* Verizon commercial led by Drew Brees (NFL quarterback), David Villas (professional soccer player), Adriana Lima (famous model), and Lebron James (NBA player) reported over 4 million science and tech jobs were available in the United States. This was highly important as youth in the commercial shared their interests to become an athlete or model for a career while the athletes shared the data of limited opportunities: 5,800 models; 2,880 NFL players; 850 professional soccer players; and 624 NBA players. Although a star Major League Baseball player was not a part of this commercial, it's important to note, according to the MLB database, 1,518 positions are currently occupied.

While some critics argue the professionals in the commercial are telling kids not to follow their dreams of becoming professional athletes or models, other critics applaud their support of a diverse workforce filling science and tech job vacancies. Now, hark back to the quote by Baldwin, "A child is formed by what they see, and the choices they have to make..." Now, meditate on the quote by Emerson, "A man is what he thinks about all day long."

Let's paint the picture—young ladies and some young men watch glamour shows, become intrigued by fashion, and are mesmerized by the attention of beauty. It becomes a captivating obsession. It's no longer a dream. Instead, this exposure becomes a sincere infatuation that transitions to a powerful imagination to become the next Adriana Lima, a world renown model. As time passes, one grows older and works emphatically to achieve this goal at all cost, in some cases, doing whatever it takes to get noticed, and blocks out other possibilities to achieve other prominent successful careers.

This cycle is the same for young men who are active in and watching sports on a continuous basis. These young men also daydream about sports, connecting to an individual in the sports world to imitate: Drew Brees, Lebron James, or David Villas, in addition to the other favorites in the professional sports arena. This too becomes the sincere passion and obsession for young men, and even some young women, to become professional athletes. The uncovering of million-dollar contracts, big houses, private jets, parties, and the allure of fame hypnotizes youth to a point of overlooking and sadly underestimating the power of the mind and the longevity of an education.

Consequently, the lack of exposure to wealthy lifestyles outside of the rich and famous deter students from taking the time to matriculate through college. Youth need to be aware of the adversity professionals overcame to be successful. It's always helpful to understand and connect with people who share their stories of struggles and life's challenges. There's a lot to learn from some of the wealthiest and brightest learners in the world today. For example, what's the story of James Dewey Watson, an American molecular biologist and co-discoverer of the DNA structure? He made over a billion dollars.

Even more, what about Dr. Ronda Stryker, Dr. Patrick Shiong, and Dr. Thomas Frist, Jr.'s stories? Why not learn how everyday working people are surviving and how they did it? How did these doctors amass well over a billion dollars in the healthcare field? Stories and background information on living professionals connect students to what they can become later in life.

Sharing the information above is not to deter youth from seeking enjoyment in modeling or athletics nor to single out a specific field, especially since accountants, engineers, chemists, and other professions can create various levels of comfortable wealth by pursuing education. Rather, this is an opportunity to share other pathways or alternative routes youth may not have known existed. Some of these things tend to be overlooked;

therefore, uncovering truths is paramount, especially since youth are formed by what they see. Because of this, increased exposure to positive images gives youth a vision to reflect on and something positive to think about becoming.

While exposure is the vision needed to activate youths' imaginations, the action driving the concept is motivation. Hence, once a student grasps onto a vision or belief, they will multiply that occurrence to reach Motivation which is *x M*.

x M is **MOTIVATION.** Motivation is the mental ability to act or move toward an envisioned thought or concept. For students, motivation is learning how to grasp things to affect behaviors and change their lives through education credential obtainment. However, being motivated is not as simple as one might assume pertaining to learning in school, especially when education is considered a convenient inconvenience to many students.

> *"Do not train a child to learn by force or harshness; but direct them to it by what amuses their minds, so that you may be better able to discover with accuracy the peculiar bent of the genius of each."*

— Plato

But where does motivation come from for a student to learn? How can a student be motivated outside of athletics? These are significant questions since students live in an era where there are 100 things other than learning in a classroom taking their attention. For starters, learners must develop a sense of control somewhere in the learning environment. Let's revisit motivation from earlier stories: Ralph, Bill, and Katherine.

For Ralph, reading and writing was something he did outside of school hours for years *on his own*. Take a closer look—Bill was so captivated by computers, he crept out of the house after dinner to go to the University of Washington campus to learn more about them *on his own*. Katherine counted everything in sight, thus learning how to hand calculate the hardest equations without help *on her own*. To make the connection to motivation clearer, please follow the next set of examples outside of structured education.

Think about how athletes learn to perform at the highest level—they practice. On any given day, they practice by themselves for hours at a time at the gym, football, baseball, or track field. The same work ethic can be attributed to entertainers and musicians. They go to studios and practice for hours and sometimes days at a time *on their own*. Collectively, not only do they believe in their abilities and talents to get better, but they're in control while being drawn to these things naturally. There is no difference—motivation is an investment in yourself.

Subsequently, inspiration comes from natural attractions. It's clear learners gravitate toward these things without coercion. Notice motivation is illustrated by how one focuses on an object that increases their value rather than depreciated materialistic items to influence behavior. For example, in the story, Ralph explored many sides of motivation beyond the scope of materialistic attainment. One form of motivation was learning how to study and prepare for exams moving forward after scoring extremely low on the SAT test. Another form of his motivation was discovering fraternities' and sororities' impact on the college campus, the community, and a student's life after graduation.

Perhaps creating more opportunities for learners to see the realities of reaching success other than athletics or entertainment will be more beneficial to their psyche. For instance, connecting students to positive images through social media outlets will help heighten their beliefs of reaching success, for visual representation of positivity can spark students' interest to complete their studies.

"Logic will get you from A to B. Imagination will take you everywhere."
- Albert Einstein

In fact, exposure has no limit on motivation, as there is not one single motivating factor to success for figuring out school. This has been supported with stories and comparisons described throughout the text. Learners must be motivated by imagining themselves becoming what they dream, just as if they were kids again: astronauts, doctors, lawyers, computer programmers, accountants, engineers, teachers, and more. This is important because motivation is omnipresent—it's everywhere!

After completing the first three steps of the equation, a student has developed a "Pathway," which is noted by the variable **Y**. In the equation,

Y was chosen because everybody's path is different. However, students must acknowledge how pathways are opened based on their skill sets in learning environments. This pathway is divided by **Destiny**.

$\frac{Y}{D}$ *is* **DESTINY**. Destiny, in this sense, is not prophecy or jargon to create any false illusions. It is to help learners understand how paying attention and taking advantage of where you are in learning settings guide the future. In fact, the geographical location, school system, environment, family situations, and other living factors are not disadvantages but advantages that shape a student's future in the end.

Therefore, it's important that educators, parents, community members, and students not overlook the way life events occur. In fact, one should always be ready to take advantage of positive connections. Remember, life happens by design, not by chance. Take heed to the signs during adolescent years as it prepares the student for adult years later. A notable example of destiny is the story of Dr. Sampson Davis, Dr. Rameck Hunt, and Dr. George Jenkins, shared in the book *We Beat the Street: How a Friendship Pact Led to Success*.

Their story includes overcoming life's hardships while growing up in the tough neighborhoods of Newark, New Jersey, in addition to being intelligent students who developed a bond that happened to put them in the right place at the right time together. To be specific, Dr. Jenkins highlighted the experience that affected their destinies, saying:

> "Thinking back to that presentation in the library makes me smile. What started out as three high school boys skipping class turned out to be the most significant event in our lives. If we had made it to the gym that day instead of the library, more than likely the streets would have swallowed us in the next few years. We never would have become doctors. Everything we needed to start on the road to success was included in one forty-five-minute presentation. And we almost missed it."

As juniors, they learned Seton Hall University had a Pre-Medical/Pre-Dental Plus Program, which sparked their interest; Hunt and Sampson remembered their encounters with doctors guiding the healing processes when they were injured, and Jenkins flashbacked to his experiences going to the dentist. Following this presentation, they discussed their options, applied to the program, and all three received acceptances to Seton Hall University. In the end, they completed collegiate studies to become doctors—Drs. Sampson Davis and Rameck Hunt both completed studies for medical doctors, and Dr. George Jenkins completed studies for dentistry.

This segment of life is often underestimated. Whether you are student in the K-12 system or on a college campus, know that things will happen for a reason, and you must pay attention to the signs. Furthermore, school is not solely meant for a student to only learn from the educators, but from everyone who has a hand in the student's success along the way. Be aware and attentive to the people and events, as they could collectively help shape students' destinies.

Y is divided by **D** for **Destiny** which opens a pathway for learners to connect with people to guide them through the school system by adding (**+ A) Accountability.**

+ A is Accountability. Accountability is the team of individuals a student creates to help them transition from high school to college to the workforce. It begins with learning how to build positive relationships with adults in the K-12 system. As the youth grow older, they spend less time with parents and more time with the outside world. While this is not to discredit the job mothers and fathers do parenting, it's a sincere acknowledgement to the smallest amount of facetime youth have with parents as they grow older.

Based on learners' needs, no matter the school system, it's best they create accountability measures at each level. It will always take a village to help learners transition successfully into adulthood. Now, as students transition to college, starting over becomes a game of chess. This in part is due to a sense of marginality and belonging on campus which stifles a college student's growth.

"I don't care how gifted you are, how talented you are, you're going to need a coach...you can't go through this world by yourself, you need people in this world, things are going to happen along the way that you can't pay for..."

- Bishop T.D. Jakes

From the sentiment noted in Bishop Jakes statement, the learning community should always consist of trusted individuals to serve as life opticians. Even more, students at every phase of education must learn how to build positive relationships with professionals. These individuals serve as **Mentors** today that become **Champions** later.

Mentoring is a positive learning relationship involving the exchange of knowledge between two people: mentee and mentor. For this example, mentoring is the pairing of a student with a teacher, athletic coach, counselor, Big Brother or Big Sister, community activist, church member, or other positive professionals. The professional serves as the advice giver, and the mentee is the learner participating in the flow of conversation. This relationship is imperative as the student learns to build trust and listening skills from a person of stature who is admired and respected. In this relationship, the adult serves as a gatekeeper, leaving a trail of wisdom and knowledge for the student to follow.

"When you see a new trail, or a footprint you do not know, follow it to the point of knowing."

-   Uncheedah,
The grandmother of Ohiyesa

However, the knowledge shared in this accountable relationship makes mentoring in the 20th century challenging, for not all mentors feel comfortable discussing personal topics and information with mentees. Because of this, students may have many mentors for several topics to share and discuss important occurrences with. Some will have a mentor for professional guidance, college help, or athletic development, while others will have a mentor to discuss personal things such as drugs, sex, money, addictions, or personal life events.

In all, it's life changing to know it's okay to have a trusted person at any stage of learning to share vital information with for guidance, for these individuals transition from **Mentors** to **Champions**. A mentor will provide a student with all the information they need to reach their goal or endeavor. But what is missing is a stamp of approval from someone who has made the connections needed for the student to advance at the next level.

"It's not what you know, it's who you know, right? Well, every time people use this quote, they leave out the third part: it's also about who knows you! For instance, if I pick up the phone and call, will you answer it? If I leave a voicemail message, will you call me back? If I send you an email, how long will it take for you to respond, or will you respond to it at all? Now think about that for a second…"

-   Dr. Don Cameron

For Katherine Johnson, it was her professor W.W. Schieffelin Claytor, the third African American to earn a PhD in Mathematics, that championed her through college to success. For Drs. Hunt, Jenkins, and Sampson, it was Carla Dickinson and her team guiding them through life, college, and into the medical profession. For Bill Gates, it was John Norton teaching him everything he needed to know about computer programming at a youthful age. For Ralph, it was Commander Copeland, Kevin Coburn, and Larome Myrick guiding him through each phase of life and education simultaneously. Overall, Mentors and Champions serve as a method for accountability that helps learners remember their purpose and informs them of which direction to take along the journey.

Not all things learned from a person will be beneficial. For this reason, a student must always think for themselves and subtract (- S) what is relevant from outsiders, coupling it with one's own beliefs and ideals to develop a **Strategy**.

$-S$ is **STRATEGY.** Strategy is bringing everything a student has learned together to reach success, which is graduation from high school and college. Throughout the years, a plethora of information is obtained to help guide students through the school system. However, an effective strategy is not obtainable when students do not remember key information, experiences, and events throughout the duration of their time in the school system.

"What you remember saves you."

\- W.S. Merwin

This simple quote is the hallmark for building a Strategy to figure out school and life at the same time by remembering the concepts explored in this text: pace, destiny, exposure, motivation, and accountability. First, focus on how to master Pace. This is done by finding an obsession with a learning symbol. Today, nonprofit organizations in tandem with colleges and universities have countless programs for students to be a part of throughout the school year and the summer. These programs are dedicated to helping students gravitate toward learning symbols—mathematics, science, robotics, computers, and writing camps. There are also nationally funded programs such as TRiO Upward Bound and Educational Talent Search, among others, located on college campuses to help students discover their Pace.

Moreover, remembering their strengths will aid them as they transition to college is a must! The plethora of classes can be confusing to one who is unfamiliar with the process. To ease the tension, students can develop a strong start by focusing on how they learn best from the Pace they set up in the K-12 system. This is invaluable as college becomes less about learning in the classroom and more about learning to live outside of the institution. Once a student has created this strategy for Pace, they must transition to Exposure.

From here, students condense everything they've seen and heard into a focus. The strategy is knowing what to do with what they have seen to envision themselves moving forward. Again, there is not a limit on Exposure, but if one overcrowds the mind and is not able to plan on one thing at a time, progress can be stifled. For this reason, take what you've seen and hone in on motivating yourself to go after what you've been exposed to using your Pace. By doing this, you have control over your Destiny as pathways will begin to open, with your academic reputation opening the doors.

Because these doors open many different pathways, guidance is needed to help make the right decisions. From here, Accountability is mandatory. A mentor who later becomes a champion will provide the information students need to unlock their potential. These individuals will pour unlimited amounts of love and nourishment into students willing to follow their lead and pay attention to the details. Students must not assume these individuals will automatically come to them—they must seek these individuals out and be consistent with the follow-up. Even more, a student must show value in the information shared during this time of accountability by illustrated changes in behavior, action-steps toward goals, and commitment to being great academically.

This information can be overwhelming, which is why students must listen and take away what they need and value at the time this relationship is constructed. It's not to say students must do and say everything their mentor or champion recommends, but rather, they should use this time to positively shape their outlook on education, life, and career goals. Take a leap and have insightful conversations about thoughts, aspirations, dreams, and goals. By doing this, you'll discover a *Tipping Point* as Gladwell posits: a maven, a connector, or a salesman that will help you be successful. A maven is someone of profound knowledge, an expert in the field, a connector who has information of whom to contact, and a salesman who can help the student deliver on results toward a goal.

After one completes their strategic approach to school, the answer to the equation is their version of what success means to them.

"To achieve a goal you have never achieved before, you must start doing things you have never done before."

-   Jim Stuart

= **<u>Success.</u>** For this story, Success is defined as graduating high school and college. There is not a focus on any particular pathway due to the many examples shared in this text: computers, healthcare, math, science, writing, law enforcement, and others. Even more, what is proposed is the fact that more people can be successful by learning how to figure out school from a calculated perspective, to be specific, using the equation in this chapter. Malcom Gladwell posits in *Outliers: The Story of Success*, "Knowledge of a boy's IQ is of little help if you are faced with a form-full of clever boys." This sentiment is also true for clever ladies, especially given that women graduate from high school, transition to college, and graduate with a credential at a rate exceedingly higher than men every year. Knowing this, the information for figuring out school is intended for all learners transitioning through the school system, K-12 and higher education.

In all, the experiences, strategies, and stories embedded in this text highlight how students can use their talents to become successful using the education system. The stories of computers, mathematics, health care professionals, in addition to reading and writing skills, undoubtedly have the power to chart a path for a quality life. And by quality, it's not about being rich or having frivolous materialistic items, but more so a lifestyle that presents comfort and financial stability through education.

"Positively embrace moments directly affecting success."

P.E.M.D.A.S.

— Dr. Ralph F. Murphy II

7

Final Thoughts

LIFE IS THE GREATEST TEACHER. In life, one must move from a learner to a thinker to an action step taker. This three-step process has been illustrated repeatedly throughout the book, but what has not been revealed are the thoughts surrounding the decisions made by Ralph early in life.

For starters, reading and writing are exceptional talents, however science and math rules the world! Therefore, please do not use this book as a scapegoat to avoid math and science in school. In retrospect, had sixth-grade not been chaotic he might've flourished in all subjects and had a more well-rounded approach to careers. For instance, he might've became an engineer, computer programmer, scientists, or a medical doctor he excelled in math and science. In this regard, please know math and science are highly important, and if given the right introduction at the right time a student could learn to love how to solve equations and master the periodic table early in life.

Also know, mentors and champions are important pieces to the one's life puzzle. Overtime, these people become family. They are needed to navigate through life, and keep in mind, it's not healthy or smart to try to go through the hardships of life alone, everybody needs someone.

On another note, when it's time for students to select universities, one should be open-minded and free, rather than fearful and setting limitations based on discomfort. The real-world, outside of education is very uncomfortable, but learning, if taken seriously, can be the easier part of life. Also know, *all* universities across the country have mentoring and accountability networks set up for students moving away from home; therefore, one must not be afraid to take a leap to become who you were destined be.

Remember education is bigger than learning in the classroom; people, environment, events, trials and tribulations. For Ralph, education is life! Life comes at students fast, there's bullying, social acceptance, not knowing how to learn, and at times being frustrated with the world to the point of giving up on yourself. Know that quitting is never an option, especially since one can develop a strategy at each level for every situation. No matter how hard the situation may seem, students must remember and believe they can think their way out of any hardship.

"Children must be taught how to think, not what to think."

— Dr. Margaret Mead

TO REMEMBER THE EQUATION FOR FIGURING OUT SCHOOL, memorize "positively embrace moments directly affecting success." This conceptualizes the importance of learning how to think using Pace, Exposure, Motivation, Destiny, Accountability, and Strategy. These concepts lead students through the education system. At the same time, these concepts provide the learning community with knowledge aiding students to develop strengths connected to P.E.M.D.AS.

By connecting students to P.E.M.D.A.S. they understand education is a treasure. Russell Conwell eluded to this in his famous lecture, *Acres of Diamonds.* In this lecture, he shared that diamonds sought after in life are often found in your own backyard. In this text, the backyard is education attained through the school system. Education helped make Bill Gates a

118

fortune and Katherine Johnson an American Hero. Education guided Ralph

through life and gave Drs. Hunt, Jenkins, and Sampson an opportunity they

didn't know existed. Of course, not every student's path will align in the

manner theirs did. Yet, highlighting the value of simplicity within education

should not be overlooked, which is why this narrative is extremely

important to students all over the world.

---

*"Education is not power, Money is not power, Information is power,
and if I gave you bad information, then I gave you bad power."*

- Dick Gregory

Without question, the information shared within this narrative

shows how to help learners navigate the school system and mature as adults

at the same time. This book serves as a guide for current and future students

in high school transitioning to college, in addition to college students

looking to learn how to graduate and enter the workforce.

While the stories are geared toward four-year universities, the

information within the text holds true for community college students as

well. The order of operations can be applied to obtain an associate degree or trade school certificate. These students need to learn P.E.M.D.A.S. the same way four-year university students do. In most cases, these students will transfer and become four-year university students that will need to learn how to navigate a new system successfully.

Overall, students, parents, professors, administrators, principals, teachers, and community organizers—the learning community—now have more tools and the power to figure out school too!

References

Angelou, M. (1997). *Even The Stars Look Lonesome*. New York: Random House.

Baldwin, J. (2017). *I AM NOT YOUR NEGRO*. New York: Penguin Random House.

Charlamagne Tha God. (2017). *Black Privilege : Opportunity Comes to Those Who Create It*. New York: Touchstone.

Davis, S., Jenkins, G., Hunt, R., & Draper, S. (2005). *We Beat The Street: How a Friendship Pact Led to Success*. United States: Puffin.

Du Bois, W. E. (2017). *The Talented Tenth*. Okitoks Press.

Gladwell, M. (2002). *The Tipping Point: How Little Things Can Make A Big Difference*. New York: Time Warner Book Group.

Gladwell, M. (2008). *Outliers: The Story of Success*. New York: Hatchett Book Group.

Greene, R. (1998). *The 48 Laws of Power*. New York: Penguin Group.

McChesney, C., Covey, S., & Huling, J. (2012). *The 4 Disciplines of Execution*. New York: Free Press.

NASA. (2018, January 15). *Katherine Johnson Biography*. Retrieved from National Aeronautics and Space Administration: https://www.nasa.gov/content/katherine-johnson-biography

Nerburn, K. (1999). *The Wisdom of Native Americans*. New York: MJF Books.

Patterson, K., Grenny, J., Maxfield, D., McMillan, R., & Switzler, A. (2008). *Influencer: The Power to Change Anything*. New York: McGraw-Hill.

Rice, K. (2009). *The Pied Piper Effect*. Bloomington: AuthorHouse.

Zachary, L. J. (2009). *The Mentee's Guide: Making Mentoring Work For You*. San Francisco: Jossey-Bass.

Author note: additional quotes were found at:

https://www.brainyquote.com/

About the Author

Dr. Ralph F. Murphy II is a native of East Cleveland, Ohio. Ralph earned a B.S. in Criminal Justice from the University of Toledo, a Masters of Organizational Leadership from Lourdes University, and Doctor of Education in Community College Leadership (CCLP) from the Roueche Graduate Center at National American University.

Dr. Murphy is an experienced and accomplished academic and student development professional in higher education. He has led student success initiatives positively impacting recruitment and persistence to completion rates for a diverse demographic of learners at The Ohio State University, Cuyahoga Community College, and Blue Mountain Community College. He has also served as a college advisor in Toledo and Cleveland Public School Districts.

Today, Dr. Murphy is the CEO & Founder Maven Scholar Consulting LLC. He is the lead facilitator presenting seminars on leadership, mentoring, K-12 student pathways to post-secondary institutions, strategies for closing the achievement gap for at-risk college students, and foster care alumni college student success.

Made in the USA
Middletown, DE
15 February 2022

61164590R00078